READING SKILLS

READING
SKILLS
second edition

William D. Baker
Wright State University
Dayton, Ohio

PRENTICE-HALL, INC., Englewood Clifs, N.J.

Library of Congress Cataloging in Publication Data

Baker, William D
   Reading skills.

   1. Reading. I. Title.
LB1050.B3 1974   428' .4'3   73-17161
ISBN O-13-762062-4

10 9 8 7 6 5 4

PRENTICE-HALL INTERNATIONAL, INC., London
PRENTICE-HALL OF AUSTRALIA, PTY, LTD., Sydney
PRENTICE-HALL OF CANADA, LTD., Toronto
PRENTICE-HALL OF INDIA PRIVATE LIMITED, New Delhi
PRENTICE-HALL OF JAPAN, INC., Tokyo

Contents

Preface

Chapters 1 through 16 of this book offer information on how to increase your reading efficiency, particularly for study material and textbooks. In conducting reading services and freshman English classes, I have found that almost every student who has read this has achieved a reading rate of 400 words per minute or better. The average student starts at about 270 and finishes at about 525 words per minute. One girl read the last chapter at 2400 words per minute and had excellent comprehension of the material.

I should like to emphasize here that extremely rapid rates are possible only for relatively easy material, for which this book was deliberately designed. Although I have written with college students in mind, I have reduced to a minimum the factors (high-powered vocabulary and long and involved sentence structure) that make reading difficult. If you hope to make the track team, it is best to increase your running efficiency on smooth, level ground. Similarly, it is best to increase your reading efficiency on material of standard, or little below standard, difficulty—the level, say of *The Reader's Digest*. Occasionally the application exercises include passages of a higher level of difficulty, to emphasize the importance of reading different levels of material in different ways. Not everything *can* be read at the same rate of speed and not everything in this book *should* be read at the same rate of speed. However, you should apply what you know about reading skills to even the most difficult materials.

Chapters 17 to 24 deal with important reading skills that are often neglected. In developmental reading programs it is not unusual for the work to stop with a consideration of the basic reading skills discussed in the first sixteen chapters. This is unfortunate, because these basic skills, important as they are, are just the beginning. You should advance beyond the utilitarian, textbook type of reading into the excitement of literature and other reading for enjoyment. The early chapters suggest means of chewing and digesting your everyday reading assignments, while the later ones are concerned with improving your literary appetite and developing a taste for good reading.

For the most part this is an eclectic book, one that culls what seem to me the best ideas and reading techniques from a large number of reading manuals and books on reading. I wish to acknowledge my indebtedness to authors who have trod this ground before me. I also owe a debt to those who have used the book and have offered constructive criticism.

I wish to thank the following for their permission to reproduce material in this book: Committee on College Reading: the excerpt from John Erskine, "The Good Reader" in *Good Reading,* published by Mentor Books; Committee on Evaluation of Comic Books: selection from *An Evaluation of Comic Books,* used by permission of The Committee on Evaluation of Comic Books, Cincinnati, Ohio; Harper & Brothers: extract from Abraham Flexner, "The Usefulness of useless Knowledge," *Harper's Magazine,* used by permission of Harper & Brothers; Little, Brown, & Company: selections from *The New Fannie Farmer Boston Cooking-School Cook Book,* edited by Wilma Lord Perkins, used by permission of the publisher; New Directions Publishing Corporation: "Constantly risking absurdity," Lawrence Ferlinghetti, *A Coney Island of the Mind.* Copyright ©1958 by Lawrence Ferlinghetti. Reprinted by permission of New Directions Publishing Corporation; Random House, Inc.: William Faulkner's Nobel Prize Aware Speech, reprinted by courtesy of Random House, Inc.; *The Saturday Review:* selections from Norman Cousins, "Speech for a Presidential Candidate," and Brooks Atkinson, "Credo of a Critic," used by permission of *The Saturday Review;* Harper & Row, Publishers, Inc.; from pages 83-84, in "Letter from Birmingham Jail"-April 16, 1963-from *Why We Can't Wait* by Martin Luther King, Jr., copyright ©1963 by Martin Luther King, Jr. By permission of Harper & Row, Publishers, Inc.

William D. Baker

Preface to the Second Edition

A new edition for a new generation. The new generation is different from the preceding one, and "things" will never be what they were. The rate of change makes getting with it even more difficult than before. Staying on top of expanding knowledge and an avalanche of information is a challenge. Although *Reading Skills* does not guarantee success, it will point the way.

How many books do you read each year? Would you like to read more books and get more out of them? If so, you have come to the right place.

How rapidly are you reading now? Fifty words a minute? Three hundred? Five hundred? If you are not sure, time yourself on one of the measured chapter readings, using the time-rate table at the back of the book to find your rate. If you practice conscientiously and follow the suggestions in the remaining chapters, there is nothing to stop you from reading anything twice as fast as you do now. Faster reading will give you more pleasure, more knowledge, and a much richer life.

For more than two decades students have been able to double their rate of reading by working through this book. You can do it, too, and when you do, you will reap the benefits for the rest of your days.

William D. Baker

READING SKILLS

Part I

THE BASIC
READING SKILLS

An important feature of this book is that each chapter can be read for two purposes: *to learn how to become a better reader* and *to develop speed.* To get the most out of this book, you should try to read one chapter a day, as fast as you can. Application Exercises—revised and expanded in this edition— enable you to practice the principles of skillful reading that each chapter sets forth. In addition, you will find questions that test your comprehension of what you have just read in the chapter-by-chapter Comprehension Checks in the back of this book.

Here is the way to use each chapter: *BEGIN TIMING YOUR READING DIRECTLY AFTER THE CHAPTER TITLE,* reading as fast as you can. Do not forget that comprehension is just as important as speed.

When you finish the selection, record the length of time it has taken in minutes and seconds. Use the Time-Rate Table (at the end of the book) to convert this time into your reading rate for that selection. Record your rate in the space provided at the end of the selection.

Immediately after recording your rate for each selection, you should turn to the Comprehension Check for that chapter in the last part of the book and answer the questions carefully—without looking back over the chapter. You should always answer a good percentage correctly, and if you miss more than three, you should not count your rate score for that day. Answer keys appear in the margins of other checks, as noted at the beginning of each one.

Record your rate and comprehension scores on the Graph of Progress at the back of the book. When you have done so, begin work on the Application Exercise for that chapter. In order to make the book more useful to you, you should work on these various materials such as practice exercises, recall devices, vocabulary quizzes, and suggestions for further study that have been placed after each chapter. Their purpose is to allow you to apply what

1

you learned to a practical reading situation. Most of them allow careful and unhurried reading and call for you to read with pencil in hand. Answer keys, when needed, appear at the end of the chapter.

The sixteen chapters of Part One cover the basic reading skills that will help you improve your reading habits to successfully meet the challenge of college study. Part Two will deal with evaluating all your reading.

Skillful Reading

The importance of the fast-moving stream of events in our modern world makes it imperative that we be well informed. Significant social, economic, and political issues, all demanding serious and openminded investigation, require more than ever before a higher level of reader enlightenment.

To advance in knowledge one must forever learn more, study more, reason more. Reading helps accomplish this; in college about 85 per cent of all study involves reading. If, as it certainly does, progress comes through study, then reading is perhaps the student's chief means to academic progress.

Since reading is of such vital significance to modern man, it is necessary for us to inquire into our present reading habits. Philosophers from Socrates to John Dewey have said, "Know thyself." Knowing how to read is a necessary part of such self-knowledge. The ability to read and the ability to choose good reading material characterize a man just as much as do his appearance and his speech. Our reading habits are as much a part of us as our ability to hold our own in a discussion or our ability to judge the difference between people. It follows that the way we read is closely connected with the way we think.

Check yourself by searching your mind for the answers to these questions. Do you read as well as you can? When you read fast do you understand what you read? Are your reading habits based on sound principles? Do you know what sound principles of reading are? Are you an efficient reader?

What is an efficient reader? He is one who can race through an ordinary novel very rapidly. His eyes move quickly over the lines of print, and his accuracy of comprehension is high. He grasps fully what he reads, and he retains for a long period what he has read. He knows that it is important to read different materials differently. He first skims a book that he intends to read thoroughly. Always he reads for a purpose, whether that purpose be sheer pleasure, information, or a combination of the two. He takes notes, mental or otherwise, on technical information or on difficult material. And of utmost importance, he concentrates intensively when he reads. Reading brings to him some of his keenest pleasures in life; he experiences a real satisfaction in doing a thing well. The more he reads the better reader he becomes, because in practicing correct habits he becomes even more skillful.

You probably believe that it is possible to read faster than you do now, but there is probably, also, a persistent doubt in the back of your mind that your understanding will keep pace. Get rid of that doubt, for it is the doubt rather than anything in the reading process itself that slows you down. You will understand just as much and in many cases more when you begin to read more rapidly. When you read rapidly, you will read in whole thoughts and whole phrases instead of word by word at a snail's pace. In this way, you will understand more completely what you read. Word-by-word reading gives little meaning; it is only when words are understood in relation to the other words in the phrase or sentence that they make sense. If you understand and accept this point, you have taken one of the first important steps toward your goal.

There are, of course, specific skills you must develop and practice in order to read well. You should, for example, always keep in mind the main idea of whatever material you are reading. To illustrate: The main idea of this chapter is skillful reading, a fact which you should remember every time you start a new paragraph. You should say to yourself, "What does this paragraph say about skillful reading? What new information will be offered here? And, how will this paragraph be related to the one before?" As you read along, you should observe and remember the important items and relate them to the main idea or to significant subordinate ideas. Further, you should go through the mental process of drawing a conclusion on the basis of the facts. Check to see if the facts actually point out something and make sense to you. Finally, you should relate what you have read to what you already know about the subject or to what you know about related subjects. If you do not apply what you read to the background of knowledge you now possess, you are reading in a vacuum.

Skillful reading is really an art. Unlike other arts, it does not demand an extremely high degree of artistic talent to be successful, but reading *is* like the other arts in that the more diligently you practice the more proficient you become.

After we finish the elementary grades, most of us never again have a formal reading lesson. Yet the ability to learn, an obviously important aspect of developing reading skill, increases with maturity. The fact, therefore, that you are now a slow reader does not mean that you must remain a slow reader. If you possess a strong and determined will to do so, *you can improve.* If you are now a good reader, you can become a better reader.

There is no royal road to skillful reading. But there are no insurmountable obstacles to it either. Be firm in your belief that you can really learn to read well and you will achieve success.

Begin immediately. Read through each chapter in this book as fast as you can. Do not make the mistake of sacrificing meaning, however, just to get a good reading rate. Of course, no matter what you are reading, comprehension is more important than speed. Yet it is well to remember that you need to shake off old, slow, inefficient reading habits as soon as you can. To do that you must make a conscientious effort from the very beginning to read more rapidly and more skillfully.

3:45

Name .... Section .... Date ....
*Record your rate here:*_____
Average rate for freshmen on Chapter 1: 270 wpm.

application exercise: chapter 1

Finding the Main Idea . . .

To apply what was stressed in Chapter 1, locate the main idea of the following paragraphs:

The Influence of Superior Minds

When you discover a good book, it seems to have a special message for you. Such a book is often worth reading twice or three times to be sure that the message sinks in. The message will change as you reread the book, meaning perhaps that at first it was not clear. Furthermore, new vistas of appreciation present themselves with repeated reading. Donald MacCampbell in *Reading for Enjoyment* says, "To discard a book [because]...it is not readily understood is as reprehensible as it would be to discard a friend because part of his discourse is over one's head." He feels it is a function of maturity to reach out and "put oneself frequently under the influence of superior minds."

Write B in front of the statement if it is too broad an expression of the main idea; write N in front of the statement if it is too narrow an expression of the main idea; write X in front of the statement if it is a correct expression of the main idea.

_B_ 1. One should not be disturbed if, on first reading, a difficult book is not clear; it is as foolish to discard it as it is to discard friends who occasionally talk over one's head.

_X_ 2. One may have to read a book more than once to comprehend it, yet the act of attuning oneself to a superior mind will help one reach full maturity.

_N_ 3. Read widely and carefully in order to reach full maturity as a human being.

Silver Dollars and Golden Words

A man, any man, will go considerably out of his way to pick up a silver dollar, but here are golden words, which the wisest men of antiquity have uttered, and whose worth the wise of every succeeding age have assured us of—and yet we learn to read only as far as Easy Reading, the primers and classbooks, and when we leave school, the . . . story books, which are for boys and beginners, and our reading, our conversation and thinking, are all on a very low level, worthy only of pygmies and manikins. I aspire to be acquainted with wiser men than this. . . . Or shall I hear the name of Plato and never read his book? As if Plato were my townsman and I never saw him—my next neighbor and I never heard him speak or attended to the wisdom of his words. . . . We are underbred and low-lived and illiterate, and in this respect I confess I do not make any very broad distinction between the illiterateness of my townsman who cannot read at all, and the illiterateness of him who has learned to read only what is for children and feeble intellects. We should be as good as the worthies of antiquity, but partly by first knowing how good they were. We...soar but little higher in our intellectual flights than the columns of the daily paper.

Henry David Thoreau, *Walden*, 1854

Write B in front of the statement if it is too broad, N if it is too narrow, and X if it is a correct expression of the main idea.

____ 1. We know only primers and classbooks, but we need to know the qualities of ancient writers.

____ 2. We value money over reading.

____ 3. We will be better people and lead better lives if we read and understand ancient authors.

A Book Carved out of Life

In his chapter on reading in *Walden*, Henry David Thoreau said that the written word "is more intimate with us and more universal than any other work of art." He wrote that books are superior to other works of art in a number of ways. He said that a book is "the work of art nearest to life itself. It may be translated into every language, and not only be read but actually breathed from all human lips—not be represented on canvas or in marble only, but be carved out of the breath of life itself. The symbol of an ancient man's thought becomes a modern man's speech.... Books are the treasured wealth of the world and the inheritance of generations and nations. Books, the oldest and best, stand naturally and rightfully on the shelves of every cottage.... Their authors are a natural and irresistible aristocracy in every society, and, more than kings or emperors, exert an influence on mankind. When the illiterate and perhaps scornful trader has earned by enterprise and industry his coveted leisure and independence, and is admitted to the circles of wealth and fashion, he turns inevitably at last to those still higher..., and is sensible only of the imperfection of his culture and the vanity and insufficiency of all his riches...."

Write B in front of the statement if it is too broad, N if it is too narrow, and X if it is a correct expression of the main idea.

____ 1. Because books are closer to life they influence us more.

____ 2. Books exert a greater influence than emperors or kings.

____ 3. A book does not merely represent life; it is carved out of the breath of life and influences us greatly.

Key to exercises in *finding the main idea:* (1) N,X,B (2) X,N,B (3) B,N,X

Survey Your Reading Habits

Suppose you went to the doctor with an irritating twinge in your right thigh, and he gave you an aspirin and sent you away. You would think, I am sure, that he was a very unprofessional doctor. You would distrust him because he had not taken the time to make a careful and thorough diagnosis. You would think him a faker for treating you without giving thought to the proper cure.

Before you begin a reading program for yourself, you should make a careful survey of your reading habits. Analyze yourself by using something like the checklist at the end of this chapter or, better yet, consult a reading specialist. Only after such an analysis will you or anyone else know what to do to make you a better reader.

It is difficult to say what aspect of your reading habits you should consider first, because these habits are conditioned by a multitude of physical attributes, mental skills, and personality factors. For example, your vision is important. If you have not recently had your eyes checked professionally, you should do so before you begin an intensive reading program. Such a program should not cause undue strain on your eyes, and if it teaches you to use your eyes more efficiently, it should in fact lessen the strain on them. Your reading can be seriously hampered, however, if you attempt to do a lot of reading with faulty vision.

Perhaps, as speed is the particular reading skill that most people want above all others, you should first test your speed of reading. Use the chapters of this book to do this. Each chapter is about one thousand words long. Simply divide into one thousand the number of minutes it takes you to read each chapter. The result will be your reading speed in words per minute.

What is the meaning of your rate as you work it out? If you are reading under two hundred words per minute the chances are that you are a word-by-word reader. You may find your lips moving, which means that you can read no faster than you can make your lips move. You will be harnessed to the speed of your lips until you can break that very bad habit. Try thrusting a pencil between your teeth or stick a knuckle in your mouth. You will find it almost impossible to lip read, and one of the worst habits of the slow reader will soon be broken.

If you read between two hundred and two hundred and fifty words per minute, you probably vocalize when you read. That is, you form each word in your throat as you see it on the printed page. This is also a very bad habit because it harnesses you to a slow speed. To discover whether or not you vocalize, place your fingertips on your throat in an attempt to feel vibrations as you read. If you do, you must make a determined effort to read with your eyes and your mind only, and try consciously not to form sounds.

Having surveyed your speed of reading, you must check other important aspects of your reading ability. One of these is vocabulary. A great deal of one's reading difficulty may be due to a limited vocabulary, which is something you can easily improve by persistent drill, discipline, and practice. When you puzzle out the meaning of a word, you obviously slow to a crawl. Perhaps knowing the meaning of words is not your difficulty. It may be that your "word attack" is not so good as it might be. Word attack means your ability to recognize the form of a word and its pronunciation. Many people, once they recognize a word, either know or can puzzle out its meaning. Their difficulty comes in recognition. If they knew how to attack the word, if they knew how to pronounce it, they would recognize it and have no trouble with it. Learning how to pronounce words by learning vowel sounds, combined vowel sounds, and consonant-vowel sounds may be what you need to improve your reading efficiency.

Check your comprehension too. Read an article from a magazine like *The Reader's Digest* or *Time*, and then have a friend ask you questions concerning it. To make it a fair test, your friend should read the article too, and ask questions that call for more than a superficial knowledge of dates or statistics. He should test your knowledge of the significance of certain dates or the implications of certain statistics. Comprehension is a process of organizing and memory, but it is more than mere recall; a grade-school pupil who has memorized Lincoln's *Gettysburg Address* may have very little conception of its meaning. Comprehension means understanding, and understanding *can* be improved, for it is not an inborn quality. A fair test of your comprehension should tell you whether better understanding of the printed word is what you need to increase your reading efficiency.

Good comprehension depends for the most part on your alertness and your ability to concentrate. If you can concentrate well, you can comprehend well, but if you are a day-dreamer, reading will be merely an eye exercise for you.

Tests developed by universities and educational agencies have been given to thousands of students to determine their reliability and validity. These tests survey your speed of reading, your accuracy and level of comprehension, and your vocabulary. You can make a better diagnosis if you take a test like one of these instead of depending on your own estimate.

Finally, remember that no one can improve his reading merely by wishing or by reading more. The first thing to do is to discover your reading weaknesses. Then make an intelligent effort to improve your reading habits. You are engaging on a self-improvement program that will make you a skillful reader—*if you work at it.*

application exercise: chapter 2

Planning Your Hourly Schedule...

An important part of your survey of your reading habits is your weekly schedule. Are you making the best use of your time? Is there a balance between work and recreation? Is time allowed for physical and social activities? Is the schedule realistic? The sample that follows is imagined. Make yours real. (Use the form on page 58.)

Answer the following questions <u>after</u> you have prepared your weekly schedule. Then revise it, if necessary, in the light of your analysis.

1. If your schedule is for a typical week, is it sufficiently flexible to allow for occasional emergencies? (When do you make up for "lost" time?)
2. Did you allow time for brushing up <u>in advance</u> for recitation and discussion courses and for reviewing notes for lecture courses? ("In advance" means an hour or two before class.)
3. Did you include a fixed time for recreational reading? (Must all your reading be preparation for a specific course?)
4. Will your plan allow you to keep your free hours really free of study activities? (Being "free" is often as important as anything else you do.)
5. Is your schedule simple enough to allow you to live in it? (Guilty consciences come from schedules laboriously made and quietly abandoned.)
6. Does your schedule allow you "reward" time? (A relaxing hour before dinner is your reward for a day of conscientious work.)
7. Is there an opportunity provided for weekly review? (Review now and avoid the end-of-term rush.)
8. Does your schedule take into account the difference between "hard" and "easy" courses? (An hour's study before and after the "hard" course will make the class more meaningful.)

9

WEEKLY SCHEDULE

Time	Mon.	Tues.	Wed.	Thurs.	Fri.	Sat.	Sun.
7-8	← DRESS AND BREAKFAST →						↑
8-9	FRENCH	PHYS. ED.	FRENCH	PHYS. ED.	FRENCH	PART-TIME JOB →	CHURCH, RECREATION, CONVERSATION, READING FOR ENRICHMENT
9-10	STUDY FRENCH	↓	STUDY FRENCH	↓	STUDY FRENCH		
10-11	ENGLISH	CHEM.	ENGLISH	CHEM.	ENGLISH		
11-12	STUDY ENGLISH	STUDY CHEM.	STUDY ENGLISH	STUDY CHEM.	STUDY ENGLISH	↓	
12-1	← LUNCH →						
1-2	MATH	CHEM.	MATH	CHEM.	MATH	↑	
2-3	STUDY MATH	LAB	STUDY MATH	LAB	STUDY MATH		
3-4	WORK ON PART-TIME JOB						
4-5	↓	↓	↓	↓	↓	SPECIAL PROJECTS, REVIEW, RECREATION	
5-6	← RECREATION →						↓
6-7	← DINNER →						
7-8	STUDY CHEM.	STUDY MATH	STUDY ENGLISH	STUDY FRENCH	↑		
8-9	↓	↓	↓	↓	COLLEGE ACTIVITY		
9-10				↓			
10-11	RELAX AND READ FOR ENRICHMENT						
11-12	↓	↓	↓	↓	↓	↓	

Reading Health

An athlete who expects to move at top speed is very careful to keep in excellent physical condition. He stays in trim and cautiously observes the training rules. Similarly, if you expect to do the best job you can in reading, you should condition yourself to do it. You cannot expect to speed over the lines of print with tired or strained eyes. Here are some simple rules for keeping in good physical shape for skillful reading.

You should have your eyes checked regularly, say once a year or so. Because your eyes are irreplaceable, you ought to give them the best possible care. If you wear glasses and have them checked from time to time, you need not worry about straining your eyes by reading excessively and at very rapid rates. Imperfect vision that has been corrected by glasses is perfectly satisfactory for reading and will not hold you back in any way. If you have been advised to wear glasses while reading, be sure to do so. It is foolish to be vain about the matter. When you begin to establish the reading habits of a skillful reader you will begin to find real pleasure in the physical act of reading.

Good lighting is important in reading. The light should come from behind or at least be so placed that it is shielded from your eyes. It should be strong enough to light the page clearly and yet not so strong as to produce a glare. Too strong a light, such as direct sunlight, puts the worst kind of strain on your eyes and tires them. With ample, clear, and well-placed illumination, you will find that you can read for hours without tiring.

The page you are reading should be fourteen to sixteen inches from your eyes, but you may find it more comfortable to read at a little shorter or a little longer distance. Choose the distance that seems most natural and most comfortable for you. It is best to hold a book in your hands or to rest it in an inclined position when you read. Avoid reading from a book that is flat on a desk or table. Not only does it cause eye fatigue, but it also makes you hold your head in a strained position.

Some people have headaches and a strained or twitching feeling about the eyes after reading a long time. Most of them could avoid this unnecessary and dangerous discomfort if from time to time they would look away from the book and rest their eyes on some distant object. Your eyes are wonderful mechanical devices, but they need your considerate treatment if they are to continue to function well. In their movements over the printed page they use up almost as much energy in a few minutes as they would in dwelling on a distant landscape for a much longer period. If you plan to spend the whole evening reading, take a short break every half hour or so. Now and then look up from your book and gaze at the other end of the room for a moment. If you do this you should never be troubled with eye fatigue. Many students who read eight or more hours a day do not experience eye fatigue because they consistently practice good reading hygiene.

There is also the matter of where not to read. Reading on any kind of moving vehicle is not a good idea. The vibrations produced by a train or bus, for example, might cause severe strain and can do irreparable damage to your eyes. In such a situation you can't possibly do a good job of reading and will probably begin to establish poor reading habits. Give up reading on trains and busses, for it is scarcely a pleasant experience and may prove a time-waster in the long run. Reading in bed is also a poor practice. It is difficult to find a good light for reading in bed, and you cannot easily manage a comfortable reading position for very long. In addition, reading in bed tends to make you sleepy, and a sleepy reader is not an efficient reader. It is foolish to read yourself to sleep because good reading requires a mind that is able to concentrate. Even if you don't intend to do "good" reading in bed and feel that "reading for pleasure" doesn't require much concentration, you still aren't helping your reading habits; when you read in bed you are breaking the training rules for efficient reading. If you are going to read, choose a fairly upright armchair or a comfortable desk chair. Then sit up and pay attention. You will find you will be much more able to concentrate and actually do a better job than if you are in a slumped or reclining position. You will also be more comfortable.

The size of print and the color and quality of the paper are other important factors in reading. Most good books nowadays are a joy to read because they are printed on dull white paper and in clear, readable type. Some cheap books, however, and many old books are printed in too small type on paper that is too gray or yellow or shiny. Avoid such books if you can. If you must read them, be sure to rest your eyes frequently while doing so. Follow the same procedure when reading microfilm on a machine in the library.

One last word about the hygiene of reading. In general the health of your eyes ordinarily depends on the over-all health of your body. Good food and plenty of sleep and relaxation are tremendously important. An alert mind, free from tension and distractions, is also a significant contributing factor to reading health. You cannot expect to move quickly and efficiently through the pages of a book if you are physically under par. The good reader is a healthy reader.

Name .... Section .... Date ....

*Record your rate here:*_____
Average rate for freshmen on Chapter 3: 310 wpm.

application exercise: chapter 3

Changing Reading Speed . . .

You have now read three chapters and have a fair idea of what you can do with relatively easy reading. Below is a selection such as you might find in an old psychology textbook. It will require slow and careful reading, a shift to a reading gear different from the one you have been using on this book. You may have to refer to a dictionary, underline certain words, jot down a few notes, and reread a passage or two. Try to master the material, time yourself to get some idea of how much of a change in reading speed you have had to make, and answer the questions at the end of the selection.

The Stream of Consciousness

The order of our study must be analytic. We are now prepared to begin the introspective study of the adult consciousness itself.

The Fundamental Fact. The first and foremost concrete fact which every one will affirm to belong to his inner experience is the fact that *consciousness of some sort goes on. 'States of mind' succeed each other in him.* If we could say in English 'it thinks', as we say 'it rains' or 'it blows', we should be stating the fact most simply and with the minimum of assumption. As we cannot, we must simply say that *thought goes on.*

Four Characters in Consciousness. How does it go on? We notice immediately four important characters in the process, of which it shall be the duty of the present chapter to treat in a general way:

(1) Every 'state' tends to be part of a personal consciousness.

(2) Within each personal consciousness states are always changing.

(3) Each personal consciousness is sensibly continuous.

(4) It is interested in some parts of its object to the exclusion of others, and welcomes or rejects—*chooses* from among them, in a word—all the while.

In considering these four points successively, we shall have to plunge *in medias res* as regards our nomenclature and use psychological terms which can only be adequately defined in later chapters of the book.

(1) When I say *every 'state' or 'thought' is part of a personal consciousness,* 'personal consciousness' is one of the terms in question. Its meaning we know so long as no one asks us to define it, but to give an accurate account of it is the most difficult of philosophic tasks. This task we must confront in the next chapter; here a preliminary word will suffice.

In this room—this lecture-room, say—there are a multitude of thoughts, yours and mine, some of which cohere mutually, and some not. They are as little each-for-itself and reciprocally independent as they are all-belonging-together. They are neither: no one of them is separate, but each belongs with

13

certain others and with none beside. My thought belongs with *my* other thoughts, and your thought with *your* other thoughts.

(2) *Consciousness is in constant change.* I do not mean by this to say that no one state of mind has any duration—even if true, that would be hard to establish. What I wish to lay stress on is this, that *no state once gone can recur and be identical with what it was before. A permanently existing 'Idea' which makes its appearance before the footlights of consciousness at periodical intervals is as mythological an entity as the Jack of Spades.*

(3) *Within each personal consciousness, thought is sensibly continuous.* I can only define 'continuous' as that which is without breach, crack, or division.

Consciousness, then, does not appear to itself chopped up in bits. Such words as 'chain' or 'train' do not describe it fitly as it presents itself in the first instance. It is nothing jointed; it flows. A 'river' or a 'stream' are the metaphors by which it is most naturally described. *In talking of it hereafter, let us call it the stream of thought, of consciousness, or of subjective life.*

(500 words)*   Rate_____.

After you have mastered the preceding paragraphs from the chapter on "The Stream of Consciousness" from William James's The Principles of Psychology (1890), take the test below to check your comprehension.

Directions: mark with a J those characteristics of consciousness James mentioned; mark with an N those characteristics James either did not mention or would not agree with.

_____ 1. Every "state" tends to be a part of personal consciousness.

_____ 2. Consciousness proceeds by constant and recurring effort, a conscious and deliberate effort of the will.

_____ 3. Within each personal consciousness, states are always changing.

_____ 4. No matter how one perceives it, the sensation of green is always green, cologne is always cologne.

_____ 5. Consciousness of self is a permanently existing idea.

_____ 6. Each personal consciousness is sensibly continuous.

_____ 7. Each consciousness is interested in parts of its object to the exclusion of others.

_____ 8. The words "chain" or "train" are as appropriate as "stream" to describe consciousness as it presents itself.

_____ 9. Changes in quality of the consciousness are often abrupt but explainable.

_____ 10. We have the means of ascertaining three kinds of thought: yours, mine, and thought-in-itself.

James's characteristics are first, third, sixth, seventh.

* Use one half the rate given in the table, letting a time of one minute equal 500 words per minute, not 1000 words per minute.

Fixations in Reading

4

Do you know what your eyes are doing when you read a line of print? Chances are that you think you do but actually don't. You assume that your eyes move smoothly along the line. According to the men who study vision and have scientific means of determining the facts, this is a wrong guess. Using an instrument like a movie camera, they have recorded the movement of "reading eyes" on a strip of film. What they have found is that our eyes, far from moving across the page in one even movement, make as many starts and stops as an automobile in Sunday traffic. They start, move a little distance, pause, start again, pause again, and so on to the end of the line.

When the examiners of filmstrips had determined this pattern of movement of the eyes, they were able to arrive at some important conclusions about reading. They reasoned that the pauses or "fixations" were made during the time when the reader was looking directly at the printed words on the line. The duration of each fixation, they found, depended on the amount of time it took the brain to translate the printed symbols into meaning. When the reader's eyes were moving, he was not looking at the words. But the time spent moving the eyes was only about one-tenth as long as the time spent on fixations.

The filmstrips indicated something else about reading. They showed that a good reader makes only about half the stops per line that a poor reader makes. More than that, they showed that the slow reader keeps going back to pick up words he did not "see" the first time. This going back, or "making regressions," meant, of course, still more time-consuming fixations. In many of the filmstrips, the slow reader was shown to be making from ten to twelve fixations per line. No wonder he was slow. The good reader polished off the same line in three to five fixations.

Study of the pictures of eye movements led the examiners to conclude that the number of fixations per line depends on two important factors. The first is the difficulty of the material. They concluded that very difficult material would mean a great number of fixations. Even good readers would be likely to make many fixations per line if they were reading extremely difficult writing. The second important factor, they decided, is the purpose of the reader. A person reading for sheer enjoyment would make fewer fixations than, say, an English instructor reading a student's theme for errors in grammar and punctuation.

Now what does all this about fixations and eye movements have to do with better reading? Just this. A slow reader or even an average reader making a great many fixations per line can be helped to make fewer fixations, thereby reducing the labor of reading and increasing his speed. Strangely enough, however, he cannot be helped by directing his thinking to the number of fixations he is making. As a matter of fact he should not think about fixations at all. His mind should be entirely on the signals offered to him by the printed page. Any outside considerations, such as the number of eye movements, should be excluded. Eye movements should become the same kind of automatic function that sending Morse code becomes for the telegraph operator or finding the keys becomes for a good typist.

Consider for a moment the similarity of reading to using a typewriter. A good typist does not think of each letter as he writes a sentence. In fact he does not think about letters at all. His fingers automatically find the typewriter keys as his brain finds the words and groups them into phrases. As soon as he begins to think about individual letters, he falters. He is most successful when he handles the letters in groups. Similarly the reader should handle words in groups, or, as we say, phrases. In doing so he will find that meaning begins to come more quickly and more clearly. Let him start considering individual words, and immediately both his speed and comprehension suffer.

In working to improve eye movement it is a good idea to read something light and interesting, something you can breeze through easily. Under *no* circumstances should you allow your eyes to go back to pick up something they missed the first time. You should concentrate intensively on moving swiftly forward. At first you may have trouble getting all the meaning, but the important thing is to jostle yourself out of your old reading habits. If you are like a good many others who have tried this experiment, you will be astonished at how much you are able to remember. An example of this is a class of freshmen students whose instructor had them read one page from a text at their own unhurried rate and tested their comprehension. Then he had them turn the page and allowed them half the time previously needed by superior readers on the first page. Again he tested their comprehension. Instead of remembering half as much in half the time, the students, to their surprise, remembered almost as much as they did before.

You will remember more than you suppose because you will be dealing with meaningful wholes, namely word groups, and therefore getting whole ideas at a glance.

A good way to increase the efficiency of eye movements is this: Read against time; then repeat the same operation against time, with a conscious attempt to increase speed. When a reader presses to get through more quickly, his eyes will be finding in familiar material new, logical, and meaningful groupings. His eyes will begin to catch clues to meaning by making groupings they missed the first time. When he tries a third, fourth, and fifth reading, he will form the habit of grouping.

The meaning is the important thing. Read to get meaning as fast as you can, and eye movement will take care of itself.

Name ....Section .... Date............
Record your rate here: 364
Average rate for freshmen on Chapter 4: 325 wpm.

application exercise: chapter 4

Finding Logical Groupings . . .

Read the following paragraph three times, thinking in terms of logical groupings. Record the number of seconds for each trial.

A former U.S. Education Commissioner, Earl James McGrath, has repeatedly asserted that greater efforts must be made to provide free tuition and scholarships for students who cannot afford college. McGrath feels that there is a pressing need for a federal scholarship program which would provide at least part of the cost of higher education. His philosophy is that public policy should allow capable boys and girls an opportunity to complete their education as fast as they are able to go intellectually. The Federal government's role should be to provide funds which will supplement those of private foundations and educational institutions for this purpose. (*100 words*)

First trial:__20_seconds
Second trial:_17_seconds
Third trial:__10_seconds

Now read the paragraph a fourth time and underline the groupings.
Practice this kind of exercise frequently by rereading articles that you find interesting in the daily paper.
Continue your practice on the following paragraphs:

Athletics at Leisure

...lately, since college athletics have won their way into a recognized standing as an accredited field of scholarly accomplishment, this latter branch of learning—if athletics may be freely classed as learning—has become a rival of the classics for the primacy in leisure-class education in American and English schools. Athletics have an obvious advantage over the classics for the purpose of leisure-class learning, since success as an athlete presumes, not only a waste of time, but also a waste of money, as well as the possession of certain highly unindustrial archaic traits of character and temperament. (*100 words*)

Thornstein Veblen, *The Theory of the Leisure Class,* 1899

First trial:__18_seconds
Second trial:_14_seconds
Third trial:__14_seconds

Now read the paragraph a fourth time and underline the groupings.

17

Poetry and Stars

The works of the great poets have never yet been read by mankind, for only great poets can read them. They have only been read as the multitude read the stars, at most astrologically, not astronomically. Most men have learned to read to serve a paltry convenience, as they have learned to cipher in order to keep accounts and not be cheated in trade; but of reading as a noble intellectual exercise they know little or nothing; yet this only is reading, . . . what we have to stand on tiptoe to read and devote our most alert and wakeful hours to. (*100 words*)

Henry David Thoreau, Walden, 1854

First trial:___*14*_seconds
Second trial:___*15*_seconds
Third trial:___*14*_seconds

Now read the paragraph a fourth time and underline the groupings.

VOCABULARY IN CONTEXT I

These words have been selected from the **Application Exercises** for Chapters 1 through 4. Match the words with their definitions by writing the number of each word next to its definition. *The answer key is on page 16.*

Words from Chapter 1		*Words from Chapter 3*	
1. vistas	*12* without fail	1. consciousness	*6* jointly
2. reprehensible	*8* wise men	2. assumption	*4* names of things
3. a discourse	*1* broad views	3. *in medias res*	*11* of one's own mind
4. antiquity	*4* ancient time	4. nomenclature	*8* based on ancient story
5. primer	*3* discussion	5. cohere	__opening
6. manikins	*9* compelling	6. mutually	*5* stick together
7. illiterate	*2* unworthy	7. reciprocal	*9* anything which exists
8. worthies	*6* dwarfs	8. mythological	*7* in exchange
9. irresistible	*10* nobles	9. entity	*1* awareness
10. aristocracy	*7* unable to read	10. breach	*3* in the middle of things
11. coveted	*5* first-grade book	11. subjective	*2* supposition
12. inevitably	*11* desired		

Words from Chapter 4

1. accredited	__science of stars
2. archaic	__antiquated
3. astrology	__to work with numbers
4. astronomy	__officially recognized
5. paltry	__insignificant
6. cipher	__fortune-telling by stars

18

Shifting Gears in Reading 5

If you are making an emergency trip to the doctor, you do not proceed at the same leisurely rate that you might use for a holiday drive in the country. You move as rapidly as you can because getting to the doctor is the main thing in your mind. During a drive in the country you take your time. You may stop now and then to examine more closely some object that has engaged your attention. Your progress is casual; you relax and enjoy yourself. On your trip to the doctor, however, nothing distracts your attention. All your faculties are concentrated on the business at hand, which is to get to a certain destination as quickly as you can.

So it is with reading: different speeds for different purposes. Although this may seem too obvious to mention, a great many people, including some who should know better, seem to ignore it. Either they plod through a Dashiell Hammett story at the same speed they would employ for an article on relativity in some scientific journal or, less frequently, they are discouraged because they can't race through difficult material at the same rate they use for light fiction.

When you change from one kind of reading matter to another, you can, and should, change your speed of reading. In fact, in order to read widely in many fields you have to read at different rates of speed. You go along in low gear until you master the difficult and unfamiliar books in a field, and then you shift to high gear as you begin to get the subject under control. For difficult passages you will sometimes have to slip into second gear, and when you run into a popularized version of your topic, you can coast along. Not all reading offers the same degree of difficulty or requires the same reading speed.

Do not ask, "How fast should I read?" on the assumption that everyone can read at some certain rate. Reading rate is strictly individual. There are no set standards; there is no ideal speed; there is no correct speed; there is no one right way. Speed varies with the difficulty of the material and the purpose of the individual reader.

Although they sometimes overlap, there are three distinct purposes that one may have for reading. Studying a textbook in sociology, one reads for information; a novel like *Moby Dick* provides enrichment of life; and a detective story offers relaxation. To some degree, each purpose requires a different method of reading.

If you begin to read a technical work on a subject with which you are not very familiar, you must read slowly and master the details, for here you are reading for information; you are reading for data that you intend to put to good use. You have to take time to master the special vocabulary of the subject, and you have to read painstakingly to understand the relation of one aspect of the subject to another. The chances are you will also have to proceed rather slowly because you will need to take notes.

When you read something like biography or history you also have to go slowly, because again you are reading for information. Suppose you read David Halberstam's book on John Kennedy, *The Best and the Brightest*, you would start slowly and proceed carefully, keeping in mind the important facts about the man and his work. But you would be able to change your speed gradually as you read more and more. You would find that you had developed a familiarity with the outstanding events in Kennedy's life. Each new book about Kennedy you later read would help you fill in some of the missing details, but there would be some repetition that would permit rapid reading.

You also read for information when you use a reference book, but in such a book you don't read through the whole thing to find what you want. For example, it would be absurd to read through an entire book on Greek history to find information on Socrates. The best method, if there were no index, would be to skim through the book until you came to the material relating to your subject. Then, reading for information, you should probably read slowly and carefully.

Speaking quite generally, the things one reads for enrichment of life are works of literature—poems, novels, short stories, plays, and essays. At least the best books of this sort are serious works of art. If you would get from them what they have to give, you should read with all the concentration and awareness at your command. Each detail, each shade of meaning, each character, each paragraph was fashioned with special care; and if you rush along, you must inevitably miss much of what the author was careful to put there for you to see.

When you are reading the ordinary adventure or detective stories you are reading for relaxation. The story probably does not give you new and valuable insight into life, but it usually is interesting enough to keep your attention. You read for the story—who gets the girl, what happens to Sam Spade, when Tom delivers the winning goal for the team. Therefore, even though you are reading for relaxation, you should read rapidly. This type of literature does not merit the time or effort of slow, careful reading.

Remember you *can* consciously change your reading rate and should set about destroying mental barriers that keep you in low gear all the time. Only when you are able to shift easily will you be able to give the various materials you read the varying amounts of time and attention that they really deserve. And only then will you be able to understand Sir Francis Bacon's famous dictum: "Some books are to be tasted, others to be swallowed, and some few to be chewed and digested."

application exercise: chapter 5

Savoring the Style . . .

Here is another selection you will need to read slowly and carefully. Though it was written by Francis Bacon in 1597 and contains a few words which may send you to the dictionary, it provides an excellent example of a terse and epigramatic sentence structure and of the force, elegance, and clarity of great English prose. Savor the style as you read it—and time yourself to get an accurate idea of how you are able to shift gears according to the difficulty of the material and the purpose for which you read.

Of Studies

Studies serve for delight, for ornament, and for ability. Their chief use for delight is in privateness and retiring; for ornament, is in discourse; and for ability, is in the judgment and disposition of business; for expert men can execute, and perhaps judge of particulars, one by one; but the general counsels, and the plots and marshaling of affairs come best from those that are learned. To spend too much time in studies is sloth; to use them too much for ornament is affection; to make judgment wholly by their rules is the humor of a scholar. They perfect nature, and are perfected by experience; for natural abilities are like natural plants, that need pruning by study; and studies themselves do give forth directions too much at large, except they be bounded in by experience. Crafty men condemn studies, simple men admire them, and wise men use them; for they teach not their own use; but that is a wisdom without them and above them, won by observation. Read not to contradict and confute, nor to believe and take for granted, nor to find talk and discourse, but to weigh and consider. Some books are to be tasted, others to be swallowed, and some few to be chewed and digested; that is, some books are to be read only in parts; others to be read but not curiously (carefully), and some few to be read wholly, and with diligence and attention. Some books also may be read by deputy, and extracts made of them by others; but that would be only in the less important arguments and the meaner sort of books; else distilled books are, like common distilled waters, flashy things. Reading maketh a full man; conference a ready man; and writing an exact man. And, therefore, if a man write little, he had need have a great memory; if he confer little, he had need have a present wit; and if he read little, he had need have much cunning, to seem to know that he doth not. Histories make men wise; poets, witty; the mathematics, subtle; natural philosophy, deep; moral, grave; logic and rhetoric, able to contend; *Abeunt studia in mores* (studies form manners). Nay, there is no stand or impediment in the wit but may be wrought out by fit studies; like as diseases of the body may have appropriate exercises. Bowling is good for the stone and reins, shooting for the lungs and breast, gentle walking for the stomach, riding for the head and the like. So if a man's wit be wandering, let him study the mathematics; for in demonstrations, if his wit be called away never so little, he must begin again. If his wit be not apt to distinguish or find differences, let him study the schoolmen; for they are *cymini sectores* (hairsplitters). If he be not apt to beat over matters, and to call up one thing to prove and illustrate another, let him study the lawyers' cases; so every defect of the mind may have a special receipt.

Sir Francis Bacon

Record your rate here: 250 (500 words in this selection)*

1. If your rate is slower here than on other material, explain why. (Use space below.)
2. Would a serious reader read <u>Of Studies</u> for information, for enrichment of life, for relaxation, or for a combination of these purposes?
3. Prepare answers to the following comprehension questions:
   a. What does Bacon mean by saying that the chief use of studying for delight is "in privateness and retiring"?
   b. What does he mean by saying that the use of studying for ornament is "in discourse"?
   c. What does he mean by saying that studies serve ability?
   d. There is no conclusion to Bacon's essay. What would his summary contain?
   e. In what sense could one spend too much time in studies?
   f. What does he mean by the statement that "studies themselves do give forth direction too much at large, except they be bounded by experience."
   g. Cite examples from your own reading of books to be chewed, tasted, and swallowed.

* Use one half the rate given in the table, letting a time of one minute equal 500 words per minute, not 1000 words per minute.

Skimming

6

The phrase "skimming along" is an appealing one, suggesting an effortless swiftness and an easy smoothness of motion. "Skimming through a book" also has a pleasant sound, and many people think that there must be an easy method of doing this kind of reading, some method that would automatically solve their reading problems. They mistake the nature of this pleasant-sounding process.

There are no mechanical rules for skimming that will enable you to do it in some easy, automatic way. There is no special way of flipping the pages or flexing your eyes; you cannot skim by reading the second word of every third paragraph; you cannot skim by reading every tenth page or by reading every fourth chapter. There simply are no such mechanical rules for skimming, none at all.

There *are* rules for skimming, however, though they are not mechanical ones. By far the most important is this: *Skim for a definite purpose.* If you know what you are looking for, if you have a question in mind and read to find the answer, if you search for specific information, you will be able to skim successfully. You know exactly what you are looking for and omit what does not suit your purpose. That is the reason and the only reason you can skim a book faster than you can read it through.

Much of the skimming you will want to do will be in books of nonfiction. In such books you should start with the table of contents. Examine it carefully to find the chapters or sections you think will best suit your immediate purpose. Decide what you will omit entirely, what you will glance through, and what you will read thoroughly. Next, turn to the particular chapters that interest you and examine the "sign posts," the chapter headings and subheadings, to note if possible where the information is you are looking for. When you begin reading a particular section, let your eyes run rapidly down the page in seeking the information you desire. When you come to a passage that appears promising, settle down and read as carefully as is necessary in order to get the full meaning. The author, a few years ago, was writing a long paper on the nineteenth-century vogue of mesmerism (now known as *hypnotism*). Having to read hundreds of books and articles, he became so sensitive to the word *mesmerism* that it literally seemed to jump at him every time he skimmed a page. When he found his "sign post," mesmerism, he would back-track and carefully read the two or three sentences before and after it to see how the word had been used in context. Skimming, thus, is not different from ordinary reading. It's just that while skimming you omit the irrelevant portions.

Suppose you wanted to find out how many Presbyterians there are in the United States. Would you flip through the pages of the *World Almanac* until you found that information? If you did you would be wasting time. The first thing you would do would be to turn to the index and look up "Presbyterians." Then you would turn to the appropriate page, run your eye down the proper column, and quickly find the figure you were looking for. You would be doing a simple kind of skimming.

When you skim any book of nonfiction you do essentially the same thing just described for the *World Almanac.* You first turn your attention to the index or table of contents. Experienced book skimmers will tell you that there is nothing more helpful to them in skimming than the index of a book.

The daily newspaper lends itself very readily to skimming. Although many newspapers print most of the news that is fit to print, not all of it is worth reading every day. Unfortunately, some newspapers do not have an adequate index, which means you must turn each page laboriously and glance at each headline to see what is worth reading. Such headline reading is skimming in one of its most common forms. After you have read a newspaper each day for a week or so, and know its various sections well, you learn to turn immediately to those parts of the paper that interest you most. You know that the business section is always in the same approximate location and that the sports columns and the "funnies" and the editorials all have their particular spot. In a short time you can learn to skim the paper with ease, because you know what you are looking for and you know where to find it.

The ability to skim a newspaper, which you have probably already developed, should be applied to skimming magazines and books as well. Magazines are easy to skim because they usually have a table of contents that enables you to decide quite easily what to read and what to skip. If you read the subtitles of the articles in a magazine, you can get a pretty good idea of their purpose and content. Take, for example, a magazine article entitled, "Give It Back to the Indians." The title is intriguing but undescriptive; it doesn't tell you what the article is about. Should you or should you not read it? Look at the subtitle: "High taxes, hot summers, and a maddening pace make Manhattan Island a perfect climate for neuroses." Here is practically a summary of the article. It reveals the purpose of the writer and even offers a clue to his humorous style of writing.

Skimming through printed matter is not as easy as skimming a flat rock over water. There is more to it than a mechanical flick of the wrist. Nor is skimming like taking the cream off a bottle of milk. It is more like scanning the shelves of a supermarket to find what you came to buy. You know why you're there, you know what your're looking for, and you look for that alone. This is skimming.

application exercise: chapter 6

Skimmimg for a Purpose . . .

Exercises in skimming are bound to be artificial since no one other than the reader can know the particular purpose he is skimming for. On the other hand, some skimming exercises can be beneficial if they give the reader practice in moving his eyes rapidly down the page and teach him to search accurately. During part of the time you spend on this practice, try to catch the feeling of your eyes selecting significant phrases. Think of your eyes moving as you read the first two selections. It is dangerous to get into the habit of thinking about eye movements, so try it only once or twice. Skim as rapidly as possible.

Baked Potatoes: Look for the reason one should break the skin.

Select smooth, medium-sized potatoes. Wash with vegetable brush, dry, and place in dripping pan. Bake 40 minutes or until soft, in a very hot oven (450°F.). Serve at once, or else break skin for escape of steam. If skins are to be eaten, potatoes may be rubbed with butter or bacon fat before baking.

Devil's Food Cake: How are the beaten egg *whites* to be added to the mixture?

Melt chocolate, add 2/3 cup sugar, 1 cup milk, and 1 egg yolk, slightly beaten. Stir and cook over hot water, until smooth. Set aside to cool. Beat egg whites until stiff; beat in 1/2 cup of sugar, and set aside. Cream butter and add remaining sugar gradually, while beating constantly. Add 2 egg yolks, well beaten. Mix and sift flour, salt, and soda and add alternately with 1/2 cup milk to butter mixture. Add chocolate mixture and vanilla. Beat well and fold in egg whites. Turn into 2 buttered and floured 7-inch square pans and bake 35 minutes in moderate oven (350°F). Remove from pans and cover with white or chocolate frosting.

Meringue Pie: Why let the mixture stand several hours?

Beat egg whites until stiff. Beat in cream of tartar and sugar, a spoonful at a time. Beat in vanilla, drop by drop, and continue beating a few minutes. Spread in buttered 9-inch pie plate, having mixture higher around edge. Bake 10 minutes at 275°F., then 30 minutes longer at 250°F.

If desired, spread with 1/2 cup heavy cream, whipped, and let stand several hours or overnight. This makes a softer, richer base. Cover with crushed, sweetened strawberries, crushed pineapple and whipped cream, or 3/4 cup apricot pulp folded into 1 cup cream, whipped and sweetened.

25

The Junto Club: How many years after it was founded did the Junto Club form a subscription library?

The Junto Club, a social and debating society, founded by Franklin at Philadelphia (1727), was first known as the Leather Aprons. The working-men who were members kept it going as a vital force in Philadelphia's cultural affairs for 40 years. A subscription library was formed by the club in 1731, the first American public library.

Insulin: Why is insulin an aid in curing diabetes?

Insulin is a hormone extract obtained from the Islands of Langerhans of the pancreas of animals (chiefly pigs and oxen), used in treating diabetes and in regulating the metabolism of glucose in the blood and urine.

Color: What is the most striking feature of color?

Color is the evaluation by the visual sense of that quality of an object or substance with respect to light (reflected or transmitted), expressed in terms of hue,chroma,and brightness.Generally the most striking feature is the hue, which gives the color its name, qualified as pale, dark, dull, light, and so on.

Simulacrum: How is it different from an exact replica?

A simulacrum is an image, something that has a similar form; a shadowy likeness of something without its substance. Carlyle said that it was time for man to "quit *simulacrae* and return to fact."

Monaco: When did the rule of the Ranier family begin?

Monaco is the smallest country in Europe, having an area of eight square miles, bounded by the French Alps and the Mediterranean. Its casino is the gambling center of Europe. The family of Prince Ranier of Monaco has ruled since 1327, and the Prince is one of the few titular sovereigns left in Europe.

Woodrow Wilson: How long was he president of Princeton?

Woodrow Wilson, the twenty-eighth President, was born in 1856 in Staunton, Virginia. After receiving degrees from Princeton in New Jersey, the University of Virginia in Charlottesville, and Johns Hopkins in Baltimore, he taught history and government at Bryn Mawr near Philadelphia, at Wesleyan in Middletown, Connecticut, and, lastly, at his *alma mater*, Princeton, where he became president from 1902 to 1910.

World War I Peace Treaty: Was Germany to be allowed an army and navy?

By terms of the peace treaty Germany agreed to restore Alsace-Lorraine to France, recognized the independence of Poland, the free city of Danzig, Czechoslovakia, and Austria. Germany also surrendered all her colonies to the Allied powers. Compulsory military service was prohibited, and the size of her army and navy was fixed. Finally, Germany was obliged to make such restitution and reparation for war damage as might be determined.

Concentration

7

To read efficiently you have to concentrate on what you are reading. You cannot read well if your mind wanders off to other things. If you are involved in a serious emotional problem or going through a nerve-shattering period of indecision, it is quite possible that you won't be an efficient reader. The reason is one we've all heard a thousand times: "I can't keep my mind on my work." Most people, however, are not so tormented by personal problems that they cannot read well if they set their minds to it. Unless your situation is distracting in some unusual way, you can learn to concentrate on your reading as well as the best.

You have already learned that when you read efficiently you read intensively. The act of reading occupies the skillful reader completely. He simply does not allow himself to be distracted by outside influences. Even if you don't consider yourself such a reader now, it is probable that if you plan to study you arrange a suitable place where you will not be bothered or interrupted too frequently. Even if you are reading just for pleasure you generally attempt to keep distracting influences to a minimum. In short, you know that good concentration depends on your ability to control and direct your attention.

If you try to listen to the radio at the same time you study a history lesson, you are going to find it difficult to give satisfactory attention to your reading. Although some investigators have shown that workers on an assembly line can sometimes increase their output if they listen to music while they work, other investigators have shown that the real reason workers produce more is because they know they are in an experiment and the experiment gives them incentive. It is true that you *can* read and listen to music, but you make it more difficult to concentrate by doing so. Even if a person could condition himself to reading in an artillery barrage, he ought not choose willingly that atmosphere. Certainly the inefficient reader fights against himself when he tries to read and listen to a quiz program. As he cannot give full attention to either activity, neither does he derive full enjoyment from either. A reader whose attention is divided cannot read at his efficient best.

As you have already noted, you can probably concentrate well enough if you seek an environment that gives you half a chance. Of course, all background noise can't be eliminated when you read. There is bound to be some. Both Thomas Carlyle and Marcel Proust tried unsuccessfully to insulate themselves from the noise and confusion of the outside world by writing in a cork-lined chamber. It is enough to try to eliminate as many really distracting influences as possible. If you can learn to lose yourself in the printed page you won't be bothered by minor distractions. Watch a twelve-year-old child read a comic book if you want to see an example of intensive reading. No minor distractions trouble him! Try to get his attention. He will not hear you until he is finished. He is quite literally "out of this world." You could drop a bomb, and he would emerge from the debris with the paper still before him—reading intensively. His taste in reading matter may not be the best, but his ability to concentrate is worth trying to imitate.

Some people find that they cannot pay attention and have a tendency to daydream when they read relatively uninteresting matter. They often find that they have gone through three or four pages without remembering a word. One cure for this is to stop reading and deliberately seek some distraction, then return to the book with renewed attention. Get up and walk around, raid the ice-box, play the piano, count your pocket change—anything. Then pick up the book and take up from where you left off. No one can tell you exactly what to do if your mind wanders when you read, because in some degree this problem is an individual one you must work out for yourself. The important thing is to do something about it, not just tell yourself, as so many people do: "I can't concentrate."

Perhaps the best general advice is: Don't mix play and work. When it is time to work, work hard. Apply yourself to your task and keep going as long as you can give the job full attention. You should be able to read for at least an hour or two without interruption. When you begin to feel that you are not getting as much out of your reading as you ought to, let up for a while. But if there is more work remaining to be done, make the rest period short. It is surprising how quickly you can refresh your mind by turning to something entirely different for a few minutes. It doesn't take long to get your mind out of a rut, and when you return to the book, you will be alert and ready to go at it with a mind refreshed.

If this suggestion does not solve your problem, there is another thing you can do. Form the habit of reading in the same place each time you read. Make this place, whether it be a table at the public library or a desk in your study, a place for "concentrated" reading. Write your letters and fill out your crossword puzzles somewhere else. After you have tried this practice for a week or two, you will find that your habits will begin to work for you—which doesn't mean, of course, that they will take over the whole process. There is still the matter of will power.

One of the principal things to remember about concentration is that you yourself must be willing to exercise the self-discipline necessary to control your reading habits. While it is true that a favorable environment is a great help, the main thing is this: Condition yourself to reading intensively.

Name .... Section .... Date ....
*Record your rate here:*_____
Average rate for freshmen on Chapter 7: 360 wpm.

application exercise: chapter 7

Focussing on Automatic Acts . . .

It is difficult to examine an action objectively if it has become something you perform automatically and without thinking. Concentration is such an act. When you are highly motivated, when you have a keen desire to accomplish a task, you direct all your powers to succeeding, and you may lose track of the conditions of sound, smell, touch, taste, and sometimes even sight during the act.

Here are a few simple tricks which require a high degree of concentration—and a relatively small amount of mental exertion. Try them to see if you can determine what conditions help you to concentrate best. (Use space for your answers and examples.)

1. Hold a watch to your ear and slowly move it away until you can no longer hear it. Then hold it at the maximum hearing distance and listen to the consecutive ticks for thirty seconds. At the end of that time you will probably realize that you can now move the watch even further away and still hear the ticks. Can you account for this?

   _____

   _____

2. Using a rubber band, fasten a paper napkin over a drinking glass. Put a penny on the napkin and in two minutes see how many different holes you can burn in the napkin with a lighted cigarette—without letting the penny drop into the glass.

   _____

3. Simultaneously move your right hand in a circle over your stomach and pat your head with your left hand. When you succeed, change hands and reverse the process; then reverse the process every ten pats. Why does this trick become easier as you practice it?

   _____

4. Look at the second hand of a watch and count the number of your heartbeats per minute.

   _____

5. In your room or study, lie on your back and hold a book at arm's length above you. How long can you concentrate on the reading before your muscles tire?

   _____

6. Read the following number once and then look away and repeat it: 55059642. Try the same with these numbers: 47247307, 05459417, 51319176, 51468938.

7. Read the following lists rapidly and pick out the one item that is different:
   robin, sparrow, bear, oriole, wren, lark (read more rapidly!)   _____
   oak, elm, maple, birch, hickory, ruler (keep moving!)   _____
   rabbit, possum, horse, mouse, eagle, squirrel   _____

Kennedy, Eisenhower, Wilson, Mailer, Johnson, Roosevelt _____

Dickens, Thackery, Longfellow, Emerson, Watt, Thoreau _____

8. Answer the following questions about overcoming boredom: (interest = concentration)

a. Are you just reading an assigned number of pages or are you trying to understand the material?

b. Challenge yourself. Can you turn the author's concepts into opposites and ask yourself why the opposites aren't true?

c. Some material needs to be mastered. Do you habitually pick out the one or two things a day that need mastering?

d. When you read, "... from the above it follows logically," do you anticipate the author's message and compare your version with the original?

_____

_____

_____

_____

_____

e. Do you ever begin by finding very elementary books about a subject? Such books can help you master basic concepts and give you a firm foundation.

f. Have you tried reading around a subject? If you read how James Watson helped discover the biological code in <u>The Double Helix</u>, it may revive a flagging interest in biology. A trip to the zoo or the botanical garden may do the same.

_____

_____

_____

_____

_____

Training in Comprehension

8

The ability to comprehend means the ability to translate printed symbols into meaningful ideas. A reader comprehends a book in terms of the ideas—gained through actual life situations and through reading—that have meaning for him. The idea of relativity, for example, has little meaning for most readers. Ideas of love or hate, however, have very definite meaning for everyone, because everyone has experienced these things. A reader's understanding is most complete when he has a rich background of experience in the subject he is reading.

It would be foolish to try to improve comprehension by enriching your background of experience in the few pages of this chapter, but it is possible to offer some suggestions for understanding better what you read.

Suppose you wish to digest a book as thoroughly as possible. Your first task will be to direct your attention to finding the central thought of each chapter, section, and paragraph by making use of all the author's "sign posts." Several kinds of these sign posts should be obvious to every reader. For example, the sign post that marks the central thought of this chapter is the title, "Training in Comprehension." Divisions within chapters may be clearly defined by subheadings, usually set off in a special type. A biology book, for example, may have a chapter entitled "Charles Darwin," with such subheadings for the chapter as "Darwin's Life," "Darwin's Work," and "Darwin's Influence." The last subheading may be further divided into "Contemporary Influence" and "Historical Influence." Another kind of sign post, not so easily noted, is the paragraph topic sentence, which is quite often the first sentence in a paragraph. If it is the first sentence, the purpose it serves will commonly be twofold: to indicate exactly how the author's thought is being carried forward from the previous paragraph and to introduce the idea of what is to follow. In other words, it concludes one unit of the author's thought and begins another. As such, it holds a key position in the pattern of sentences on the page. It is, therefore, a sign post for which we should look. Determining the author's topic ideas is crucial to good reading comprehension.

Another suggestion which can lead to more complete understanding of what you read is this: Sift ideas. That is, try to find what is significant and what is not. A good reader working for thorough understanding makes a constant attempt to find the author's main ideas and to relate the minor ideas to it. In order to decide what is worth remembering, he separates the frills—the unimportant facts and details, which are offered only as extra evidence to reinforce a point already made—from the main ideas. Someone has said that the sign of a truly successful executive is an empty wastebasket at the start of a day, and a full one at the end. Similarly, a successful reader discards the unimportant things he reads.

Suppose an author begins a paragraph like this: "Youth, as a rule, has an immense reserve of strength and thus has the ability to cope with changed conditions." This, of course, is a generalization, and it will need facts and illustrations to back it up. Suppose that, later in the paragraph, the author wrote, "On treacherous White Lake, three teen-age campers were able to cling to their capsized boat for twelve hours." This is an illustration offered as evidence of the truth of the statement about youth. When the two statements are separated and discussed, as they are here, it is easy to see the relationship between them. A good reader constantly finds such relationships between main ideas and details. Poor readers, on the other hand, rarely bother to do so. As a result of this failure to train themselves, they not only misinterpret the author's meaning and thereby reveal themselves as poor readers, but they also carry into their everyday lives a mass of misconceptions and wrong ideas.

The man who forms his opinions mostly on the basis of what he reads in newspaper headlines is an example of a reader who often fails to make logical connections between facts and generalizations. Headlines are "eyecatchers," that is, in a limited number of words and in an appealing or even sensational manner, they must tell the reader what is newsworthy. Thus, they sometimes distort the news by making generalizations that the facts may not support. For instance, when a doctor told a public health group the results of an attempt to help autistic children, the headline and the first three paragraphs of the news story that treated the doctor's speech read as follows:

Autistic Children Can Relate

Chapel Hill, N.C.—Seated beside the therapist, five-year-old Mary squirms, lolls, bobs her head, and focuses on thin air. She is autistic, unable to relate to people or things.

Then the therapist calls her name until Mary looks at her. Touching her lips, the doctor pleads with Mary to touch her own lips and say the word "lips." Mary finally obeys.

Mary's parents observe unseen in another room. They too are part of her therapy.

The reader who stops there forms his opinions on ideas unsupported by facts. The parts of the article he has read may lead him to think that there may be a sure treatment for autistic children. Yet the article goes on to say that because of the severity of the problem most of the children will never "make it" in the normal sense. The headlines and beginning paragraphs lead one to one opinion; the facts, which follow, lead to another. To comprehend the whole article the reader needs to examine the relationship between facts and generalizations.

Good comprehension demands that you think of reading as a constant searching out of meaning and that you sift and evaluate and select among the facts and ideas on a page—noting what is most relevant, discarding the unneeded.

Name .... Section .... Date............

*Record your rate here:*_____
Average rate for freshmen on Chapter 8: 370 wpm.

application exercise: chapter 8

Finding Signposts . . .

Read rapidly and find the main topic of each of the following paragraphs:

Tecumseh's Speech at Vincennes in 1810. "Brother, since the peace was made, you have killed some of the Shawnees, Winnebagoes, Delawares, and Miamis, and you have taken our land from us, and I do not see how we can remain at peace if you continue to do so. You try to force the red people to do some injury. It is you that are pushing them on to do mischief. . . ."

peace

Associated Press dispatch, December 18, 1903. "The machine flew for three miles and gracefully descended to the earth at the spot selected by the man in the navigator's car as a suitable landing place. . . . The navigator, Wilbur Wright, . . . started a small gasoline engine which worked the propellers. When the end of the incline was reached the machine gradually arose until it obtained an altitude of 60 feet."

The Machine flew

Henry David Thoreau's journal entry for January 26, 1841. "A man's wealth is never entered in the registrar's office. Wealth does not come in along the great thoroughfares, it does not float on the Erie or Pennsylvania canal, but is imported by a solitary track without bustle or competition from a brave industry to a quiet mind."

Wealth.

William Hazlitt's opinion of Voltaire's Candide. "*Candide* is a masterpiece of wit. . . . It is in the most perfect keeping, and without any appearance of effort. Every sentence tells, and the whole reads like one sentence."

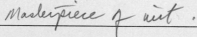

Masterpiece of wit.

William James on habit. "Every one knows how a garment, after having been worn a certain time, clings to the shape of the body better than when it was new; there has been a change in the tissue, and this change is a new habit of cohesion. A lock works better after being used some time; at the outset more force was required to overcome certain roughness in the mechanism. The overcoming of their resistance is a phenomenon of habituation."

John Moreley's opinion of Voltaire's Candide. "Rapidity of play, infallible accuracy of stroke, perfect copiousness, and above all a fresh and unflagging spontaneity, combine with a surprising invention, to give [Voltaire's work] a singular quality, of which we most effectively observe the real brilliance by comparing them with the too numerous imitations that their success has unhappily invited since."

Henry David Thoreau's journal entry for February 6, 1841. "...the value of the recess in any public entertainment consists in the opportunity for self-discovery which it offers.... In the recess the audience is cut up into a hundred little coteries, and as soon as each individual life has recovered its tone and the purposes of health have been answered, it is time for the performances to commence again."

Associated Press dispatch, December 18, 1903. "There are two 6-blade propellers: one arranged just below the frame so as to exert an upward force when in motion and the other extends horizontally from the rear to the center of the car furnishing forward impetus. Protruding from the center of the car is a huge fan-shaped rudder of canvas, stretched upon a frame of wood. This rudder is controlled by the navigator and may be moved to each side, raised or lowered."

Remembering What You Read   9

Some people seem naturally able to remember a great deal; others labor to acquire the skill. We hear of men who can memorize whole pages of a telephone book, and at the opposite extreme we know of others who have trouble connecting a name with a familiar face. Do you sometimes read an article and next day find yourself unable to recall its important details? Do you find yourself remembering an incident or a character in a story and forgetting everything else about the story? If you don't you are unusual. Most of us are unable to recall what we read nearly so well as we would like to. Let us consider, therefore, some things we can do to improve our ability to remember what we read.

One important thing to do is to look for the thread of unity that ties a book together. If, for example, you are reading a book on the Civil War you may find that the dominant, unifying intent of the author is to demonstrate the economic basis of that conflict. A book on the New Deal might have the quest for security as its primary thesis. Keep this constantly in mind, then, as you read the book. When you come across dates, names, locations, or definitions, read with an awareness of their mutual relationship and of their emphasis on what it is that the author is trying to do. Make the connections that bridge the gap between isolated details and the main point. A fact that may be relatively meaningless by itself, and therefore difficult to remember, will often stick forever in your mind once you recognize its relation to some important general idea.

The advice just given is not always easy to apply, as, for example, in reading a history book full of names, dates, and events. If you are reading such a book, you can help your memory to retain the details by using the visual aids in the book. Carefully analyze the maps and diagrams until you feel you have mastered their meaning. To do this, keep the map in front of you as you read, try to connect people's names with places, and try to relate the dates of events that are unfamiliar to dates of events you already know well. For instance, because 1492 is a date every American knows as well as he knows his name, it would be easy to remember that Greek was first taught at Oxford in 1491. It is worth repeating that to remember facts, find relationships.

Another suggestion for remembering is to do what the true murder-mystery addict never does: Look at the end of the section or of the chapter or of the book. Reading an author's conclusion or his summary will help you get an idea of how various parts fit into a whole. If you are reading an abstract discussion and it seems to become more and more difficult, glance at the ending to find out where the author expects you to be when you have finished. When you know what the goal is, you will better remember details along the path that leads to it. You will also have a greater incentive to travel over that path. If, on the other hand, you blindly persist when you do not understand, stubbing your intellectual toes, so to speak, at every rocky step along the way, you will be forcing your memory to work in a way that is unnatural and for which there is usually no need.

Consider an illustration of how a conclusion can aid in understanding the details on which it rests. If you are told that all of man's actions depend on the will of God, you perhaps nod your head and cease to think about it further. Or if you are told that it is impossible, logically speaking, for a created being to impose its will on whomever created it, you smile apologetically, resolve to brush up on your theology, and forget the whole thing. But you would neither nod your head nor smile apologetically about these matters if you were a puritan. You would think about them constantly, because religious doctrines and the details of belief which led to those doctrines were a driving force in the life of every Puritan—man, woman, and child. When the followers of John Calvin preached a message of predestination to the Puritans, they sat up and took notice. Some of the details of belief that led to the idea of predestination were that God controls all men rigidly, that no acts of man entitle him to Heaven, and that all but the elect are doomed to the fiery pits of Hell. Now, Calvin was working with details of belief which Christians had always professed, yet when he applied them with an unbending logic, the details became terribly significant to his followers. The point is this: No one had any difficulty remembering the fine points of the Calvinistic doctrine because they were understood in relation to a highly significant and central idea, an idea that controlled people's lives.

Should you have difficulty finding the unifying idea in something you are reading, you will be better off in choosing a wrong theme than in choosing nothing at all. When you read with a misconception of the main idea, you will find yourself challenging and questioning the author at every step. You will begin denying the value of the details, until your memory is pushed far enough by the act of rejection and denial to force you to find the author's true purpose. Immediately the things you couldn't fit into the jigsaw puzzle will begin to fall into place, and you will remember them partly because it was so hard to work them into the pattern in the first place.

Provide your memory with a framework in which it can work. Only in this way will you begin to establish the unending system of relationships—parts to whole and whole to parts—which is essential to good reading memory.

Name ....Section .... Date.............

*Record your rate here:*_____
Average rate for freshmen on Chapter 9: 390 wpm.

application exercise: chapter 9

Using Mnemonic Devices . . .

A mnemonic device is an aid to memory. Like a string on your finger it reminds you not to forget; not only that, it offers specific help. Mnemonic devices may be words, sentences, rhymes, and other formulas that associate a complex principle or body of fact with a simple statement that is easy to remember.

Examples of mnemonic devices:

1. Thirty days hath September . . . Can you finish the rhyme?
2. The i-e spelling rule. Can you state it correctly?
3. The rule for doubling the final consonant in spelling. In this instance the rule itself is the mnemonic, because it is easier to learn the rule than it is to remember the spelling of hundreds of words to which the rule applies. Although the rule sounds complicated, it is easy to remember if you devise a mnemonic for the rule! A useful mnemonic for the doubling rule in spelling is one that takes an example from each category of the rule and constructs a sentence, thus: "He **benefited** by **omitting cleared paintings**." Now the rule: There are two main divisions—A and B.

Rule A: Single-syllable words (five parts to the rule):
1. For words of a single syllable
2. ending in a single consonant
3. preceded by a single vowel,
4. double the final consonant
5. before adding a suffix beginning with a vowel.

Application: **plan** + **ed** = **planned** (but **clear** + **ed** = **cleared**; **paint** + **ed** = **painted**)

Rule B: Words of more than one syllable (six parts to the rule):
1. For words of more than one syllable
2. ending in a consonant
3. preceded by a vowel,
4. where the accent is on the last syllable,
5. double the final consonant
6. before suffixes beginning with a vowel.

Application: **refer** + **ed** = **referred** (but **open** + **ed** = **opened**)

Reverse of rule B: In learning a mnemonic it is often just as helpful to be able to apply it in reverse—when the mnemonic is a rule.

a. If the word ends in a consonant-vowel (c-v), as in **rate**, or in two vowels and a consonant (v-v-c), as in **clear**, or in a vowel and two consonants (v-c-c), as in **paint**, do not double the final consonant. Remember, the word has to end in v-c.
b. If the accent is not on the last syllable, the final consonant is not doubled, as in **open, opened**.

Exceptions: (just three) allow, allowing; equip, equipped; question, questionnaire.

Test

To test your understanding of the rule and the theory of mnemonics, apply the doubling rule to the following words:

transfer	refer
stop	begin
excel	trap
occur	avoid
fate	confer
ship	propel

Forming Habits

How are one's habits formed? Psychologists do not know exactly but agree that habits have something to do with the nervous system. The assumption is that a stimulus, let us say the sight of a printed word, begins a nervous impulse that, starting through the eye, runs its course to the brain. The impulse, finding its way by some route through the nerve cells, leaves a path that offers less resistance to the next impulse. When the next impulse is started, it makes the path still easier to travel, so that succeeding impulses follow the path very readily, finally even automatically. Thus, a habit is formed.

You may ask what determines the path of the original nerve impulse to the brain. Again, no one knows exactly. If your house is exactly halfway between two letterboxes, why is it that you choose one rather than the other the first time you mail a letter? As both boxes are equally near, there is no particular reason for choosing the one, but the first act establishes the habit, and except for some special reason, you always use the same letterbox in the future. You started that habit simply because there was no reason why you should not, and unless you learn a good reason for changing it, you will keep it. So it is with reading. You have acquired certain reading habits, and unless you are convinced that there are better habits of reading, you will keep the ones you have.

Consider what habits do for us. They direct our movements and lessen fatigue. Watch a child who is learning to tie his shoe, and you will see the value of habits. If movements did not become automatic through practice, it would be continually necessary to repeat the child's trial-and-error method. Habits lessen fatigue because the nervous system tends to do things in the simplest possible way, the way that requires the least energy. Therefore, once we find an easy way of doing something, we conserve energy by establishing this easy way as a habit.

Because habits make our movements automatic, they first reduce and then eliminate the need to pay attention to the performance of various acts. Consider how difficult it would be to pay attention to everything we do when we operate a car. When we are learning to drive, we think of turning on the ignition, stepping on the starter, pushing in the clutch, shifting the gears, and regulating the gas. If we had to continue concentrating on each mechanical aspect of driving, we would be poor drivers indeed. Fortunately, habit takes over, and we soon find ourselves paying more attention to other drivers, which is as it should be.

But though habits are useful things, they also present a serious difficulty. Practice, we are told, makes perfect; but, as someone has remarked, it would be truer to say that practice makes permanent. If you are a word-by-word reader and you repeat the practice until it becomes firmly ingrained, you are in the unfortunate position of possessing a habit you would be far better off without and one that you will not be rid of until, through practice and discipline, you acquire another habit in its place.

In order to possess good reading habits you must consciously set about acquiring some and avoiding others. You should, for example, attempt to form the habits of concentrating intensively and of seeing words in groups, but you should not, as we have said before, allow yourself to fall into the habit of a single reading speed for all kinds of material.

Forming good reading habits is fairly simple if one really has the desire to do so. Let us consider the case of Mr. X, who wanted to learn to read faster. He was an average reader when he started his course of training, which means that his speed was about three hundred words per minute. During the first few days of the course, he showed a gradual but definite increase, and about the tenth or twelfth day there was a considerable jump in speed. Then the increase was gradual again until the eighteenth or twentieth day, when the speed began to level off to about eight hundred words per minute. It might have been possible for him to increase his speed even more, but the chances are that a significant increase from that point would take two or three times as long to achieve. Mr. X was satisfied with his newly acquired rate of reading and had little desire to improve any more; for this reason it would take longer now to increase his speed.

If Mr. X's daily rate of reading was plotted on a chart, the line would resemble an S curve. The gradual increase in the beginning might be attributed to his difficulty in overcoming old habits of reading, and the big jump halfway through the twenty periods of practice probably would represent his final throwing off of these old habits and his acquiring of the new. Had he stopped practicing after the tenth period, it is quite probable that he soon would have reverted to the old habits. Since he continued his work, however, he was able to give the new habits a chance to become automatic. And by the time he had practiced reading at the increased speed for six or eight periods, the new habits were just about as automatic as the old ones used to be.

Not all readers are exactly like Mr. X, of course, but many follow a similar pattern of learning in their attempt to increase speed. The thing to remember about Mr. X is that he had a strong desire to better his speed, he practiced regularly, and he did not give up until he was satisfied that his new habits had become automatic.

5
10
9
1
6
4
2
8
3
7

3
4
1
8
13
2
11
6
12

15
5
14
10

7
9

*Record your rate here:*_____
Average rate for freshmen on Chapter 10: 400 wpm.

application exercise: chapter 10

Checking on Changed Reading Habits . . .

If you followed the suggestions in Chapter 2, you checked your reading habits when you started this book. Now, to see if your reading habits have changed since you began this course, answer the questions below.

1. How much time does it now take you to finish your reading assignments?
   _____

2. How accurate is your comprehension now? _____

3. How much time per week do you spend reading now? _____

4. How much of a difference in rate is there now in your reading of difficult and easy material? _____
   _____

5. Is there a difference now in the amount of material you read per week?
   _____

6. Have you established a favorite place to do your reading? _____

7. Do you now tire less easily when you read? _____

8. Do you sense that you are reading groups of words effectively? _____
   _____

9. Do you make fewer regressions? _____

10. Can you now concentrate better when you read? _____

11. Can you remember what you read more easily? _____

12. Do you now enjoy reading more? _____

13. Do you feel your over-all reading efficiency has changed? _____
    Explain in a sentence or two why you think it has (or has not).
    _____
    _____
    _____

Note: If you feel there has been no improvement in your reading habits since you began this course, you should probably check with your instructor and work on your own motivation (promise yourself a better reward.)

VOCABULARY IN CONTEXT II

These words have been selected from the **Application Exercises** for Chapters 5 through 10. Match the words with their definitions by writing the number of each word next to its definition. *The answer key is on page 40.*

Words from Chapter 5

1. disposition	__inclination
2. marshaling	__worked out
3. sloth	__block
4. affection	__taking care of
5. humor	__cutting overgrowth
6. pruning	__pretence
7. confute	__bringing together
8. wit	__lively intelligence
9. impediment	__laziness
10. wrought out	__speak against

Words from Chapters 6 and 8

1. (to) cream	__living
2. fold in	__isolated substance
3. vital	__soften by stirring
4. extract	__amends
5. metabolism	__exceptional
6. titular	__mix gently
7. *alma mater*	__abundance
8. restitution	__bearing a title
9. cohesion	__free or causeless
10. phenomenon	action
11. copiousness	__moving force
12. spontaneity	__bodily processes
13. singular	__small groups
14. coteries	__observable fact
15. impetus	or event
	__one's school
	__a sticking together

Typographical Aids and Word Signals

When you have a long trip to make, how foolish to walk rather than to use an auto, train, or airplane. When there is a letterbox just around the corner, how foolish to carry a letter to a faraway friend. When the miracle of electricity is at your fingertips, how foolish to read by candlelight. When a book has been set up with mechanical aids to help you, how foolish not to use them. This chapter concerns these mechanical aids for the reading we do in college texts, but the ideas may often be applied to pleasure reading too.

"Mechanical aids" refers to such things as different sizes and kinds of type and to punctuation marks—the various signals that serve as road signs, so to speak, for the reader and guide him to the author's meaning. Modern writers of fiction are acutely aware of these special devices in reading. In books like William Faulkner's *The Sound and the Fury* or John Dos Passos' *U.S.A.*, the reader must understand what the author is trying to do with unusual typographical devices. Whole sections are printed in italics, for example, to show that they exist in the minds of the characters or are not expressed aloud. A great many modern authors use italics to show dream states and to suggest a stream of consciousness in writing.

The mechanical aids used by Dos Passos, Faulkner, and other modern authors are more than matched by the men who write textbooks. Some aids in textbooks, such as titles, chapter headings, and subheadings, each in its own distinctive type, are obvious. Others are not so plain, for example, special words like *however, moreover,* or *nevertheless* that refer to ideas that have come before or will come after, or words like *primarily, chiefly,* or *especially,* used to stress the value of important points. These words will be discussed shortly.

Modern techniques of printing make it easier to read today's books. Sizes and shapes of type, such as boldface, italics, and capitals, are very important. Boldface is type that has thick, heavy lines, and it is used for emphasis. **Boldface looks like this.** You can usually find boldface printing in chapter titles and directions. Italics are also used for emphasis and are different from boldface in that the lines are thin, slope to the right, and are made to look like handwriting. *Italics look like this.* They often stress special words or indicate pitch of a word. Titles are usually printed in italic type. For a very strong emphasis CAPITAL LETTERS are used.

Various other devices, such as the method of punctuating, serve very well to draw your attention to an author's meaning. If he uses quotation marks around words, for example, the author intends to lay special stress on those words. When he sets off a phrase with a dash or with parentheses he often means to imply that these phrases are remarks "by-the-way" or afterthoughts. Such marks as the exclamation point, question mark, colon, and semicolon all have definite meaning. If you are uncertain about what any of them means, study a manual of usage so that you know the meanings at sight. To make the author's meaning clearer, pictures, charts, and diagrams are often put in, usually where words, by themselves, would fail.

But those who write textbooks must, of course, rely mainly on a good choice of words to convey their ideas. The Chinese proverb, "A picture is worth a thousand words," and the modern adaptation, "The right word wisely chosen is worth ten thousand carelessly chosen words," are equally true. At any rate, it is with words that we deal most as readers, and certain of them deserve special mention. Words to show contrast, like *however* or *yet*, keep guiding the reader to the author's meaning. Reference words and phrases, such as *this, that, these,* and *those,* like the contrast words relate one part of the sentence to another. Words like *moreover, further,* and *besides* tell us to look for something more. Phrases that contain numbers (*two* ways, *five* points) tell us how the thought is to be set up, and words like *in particular* and *especially* are often used to indicate a main point.

The outline is often used to show how a subject is to be treated. Subdivided under numbers or letters, the main elements in the argument stand apart from each other and are distinct. Usually main ideas are set off by Roman numerals and minor ideas by capital letters, Arabic numerals, and lower-case letters. The outline is a display, clear and concise, of the main points of the text. Whenever the author provides one, study it well. You will find it a great help in understanding what you read.

If a text is not outlined in an obvious way, all you need to do is examine the order of the paragraphs to see how the author divides his ideas. In well-written texts you can often get a fairly good idea of the author's purpose by reading the first and last paragraphs of a chapter or section, because usually a good writer will tell you where he is going and where he has been.

As your object in reading is to find the writer's complete meaning, you should examine the ways authors mark what they have to say. To neglect these ways is to fly blind.

Remember, however, that we are not suggesting here a substitute for thorough reading. Using the many types of reading signposts is valuable but can never take the place of a careful study of the text itself.

application exercise: chapter 11

Finding the Guide Words . . .

Read these paragraphs, underlining the words that guide the reader.

Taking Objective Exams

Educators are turning more and more to the objective examination as a means of measuring ability. Many professors feel that an objective question can get at the heart of a matter more precisely than an essay and that it does a fairer and clearer job of distinguishing between good and poor students. The mechanics of taking an objective examination are relatively easy, and students are tested for what they actually know, not for how they can express it. There is, however, a sound method of taking an objective examination that eliminates almost every possibility of getting tangled with mechanics. First, read the directions carefully and allot your time in proportion to the weighting of the questions. Second, go through all the questions and answer only those you are positive you know. Third, go through the list again and answer those you are reasonably sure of. Fourth, work on the questions that stump you, making a careful guess rather than leaving a blank. Fifth, review all the questions and make changes only if you are positive that the first answer was incorrect.

Preparing for an Exam

When I was in graduate school, I took a course in American history. The professor was an excellent teacher, but he was also a stiff marker, and it was particularly important that I do good work for him. Here's how I prepared for the final examination. I took careful and systematic notes at the daily lectures. I tried to get everything into them: general statements, relationships, and important principles; but I concentrated most on getting names, publications, places, dates, and examples. I think I wrote about one thousand words an hour during those lectures, and I often regretted that I couldn't take shorthand. Fortunately, I had a free hour following them, so I went to my desk and worked over the notes right away. I looked up the names, dates, and publications in my reference books, trying to find out more about them so they would stick in my mind. At the end of the week I would type the lecture notes and review them with red pencil in hand. Four or five times during the course I typed the notes I had taken from the assigned readings and correlated them with the lecture notes. Where the teacher had mentioned one fact or example to back up a generalization, I tried to supplement it with as many as I could find from the readings. When it came time for the final review, I found that the tasks I had worked at daily (reviewing

45

the lecture notes), weekly (putting the week's notes together), and monthly (integrating lectures and readings) had prepared me fairly well. During the last week, I went to the library and got the past exams that had been placed on file there. I didn't worry about answering the old questions but rather concerned myself with the type of material the questions seemed to search for. Then I made out my own exam and carefully prepared the answers, including as much factual data as I needed to support my general statements. That week I spent one period a day in review. I went to bed early the night before the exam, confident that I had learned enough about one period of American history to write a textbook if need be. The exam was a fair one, and my only problem was selecting the best facts and examples to put down on paper. P.S. I passed.

Comprehension Checks . . .

Taking Objective Exams

1. Professors feel the objective question has two advantages. What are they?
2. List the five steps in taking an objective examination.

Preparing for an Exam

1. What did the student include in his notes for the American history course?
2. When did the student look up names and dates in the reference books?
3. What did the student do with the typed lecture notes and the typed notes from the assigned readings?
4. How did the student study during the final week?

Key Abbreviations . . .

One type of word signal that can easily be classified and learned is the frequently used abbreviation. E.g. is an example. It means for example. Look up the meaning of the following abbreviations frequently used in footnotes:

TEST

i.e. *that is*	c.f. *Compare*	bf. *boldface.*
op. cit. *in the work cited*	passim *here and there*	do. *ditto*
loc. cit. *almost in the place cited.*	etc. *and so on*	ff. *following*
ibid. *in the same source.*	et al. *and others*	viz. *namely (that is to say)*

Words, Words, Words

12

Your ability to comprehend and critically evaluate what you read depends on your knowing the meaning of a large number of the words you see in print. A person who reads well at the adult level must inevitably possess a sizeable vocabulary.

You can enrich your vocabulary in various ways, but perhaps the best way is through your ordinary reading. There is good reason why this is a better way than studying word lists as many people do. A word standing by itself in a list does not offer clues to its meaning as does a word standing in a sentence. You can learn about an unknown word in *context* by relating it to the meaning of the words that surround it. Take, for example, the word *context*. You can easily arrive at its meaning by noting the words around it. You note also that these surrounding words *relate to it in meaning*. Thus you have discovered that *context* means "surrounding words that are directly connected to a given word and that add to its meaning."

Learning words in context is, as we have said, the best, and often the easiest, way to improve your vocabulary. But no matter how true this may generally be, you will find that you are frequently led to the dictionary. The habit of using the dictionary is absolutely necessary for a person who expects to have a rich and varied vocabulary. Browse occasionally in a good dictionary. Believe it or not, your dictionary can provide many an evening of diversion, diversion that pays valuable dividends.

The dictionary will usually offer a choice of several meanings for a word, allowing the reader to select the meaning that is best in each circumstance. First try to determine its meaning from the way it is used in your reading; then check your work with the dictionary.

However, you should not overlook words that come to you from sources other than reading. Do not hesitate to stop someone who uses a word you do not know and ask him what he means. This may seem an embarrassing procedure, but you will find that nine times out of ten the person will respect you for asking. And it is better than making a wrong guess about a word's meaning. In fact a hazy notion of a word meaning may be less helpful than none at all. Hucksters and "confidence men," and even some unscrupulous politicians try to confuse the public by using words that mean one thing but sound like something else. A senator who was running for re-election was accused by his opponents of deliberately living a life of celibacy before marriage. The voters evidently listened to the words "accused" and "deliberately" and felt that the key word to follow would be unfavorable to the senator. When they heard "celibacy" followed by "before marriage" they were mislead into thinking the senator was a scoundrel and he was not re-elected. His opponents guessed that very few would know that the exact meaning of celibacy was an "unmarried state," and they fooled those who make a habit of settling for a hazy notion of a word meaning.

A good stock of exact meanings will give you a distinct advantage in reading, for you will be able to criticize an author more intelligently. Learn to test the value of an author's choice of words and challenge him at every step he takes to mold his reader's opinion. It is not enough to *have* a good vocabulary. It is not enough to understand. It is important to use your understanding of word meanings as a *tool of criticism*. Become aware of words used like a broadsword to drive home points emotionally in contrast to those used as a rapier, making deft, rational thrusts at the reader's mind. Two examples will point up the difference between the two techniques, and both will serve to show that it is not necessary to use five-syllable words to say something profound or moving.

Norman Cousins, in an article in *The Saturday Review,* relied on the rapier technique to appeal mainly to one's reason. Note the way he repeats simple words like "people" and "hold" to emphasize his points. "The test of a democracy in a time of crisis," he says, "is measured not so much by the confidence of the people in their government as by the confidence of the government in the people." He continues, "No greater mistake can be made by leaders of a free people than to hold back in what has to be done because of doubts they may hold that the people may not be ready for big decisions. This is to hold the people lightly."

And here are words used as a smashing broadsword with a strong appeal to emotions. Patrick Henry said, "Gentlemen may cry peace, peace—but there is no peace. The war is actually begun! The next gale that sweeps from the north will bring to our ears the clash of resounding arms! Our brethren are already in the field! Why stand we here idle? What is it that gentlemen wish? What would they have? Is life so dear, or peace so sweet, as to be purchased at the price of chains and slavery? Forbid it, Almighty God! I know not what course others may take; but as for me, give me liberty, or give me death!"

Your ability to *use* your understanding of word meaning is as important as having a large stock of word meanings. One's whole life is a process of learning, and no one will discredit you for having an interest in words. An important basis for judging a person ought not to be his present level of achievement, but rather how actively he is taking steps to better himself. Develop a real curiosity about words, and you will have taken a great stride toward successful reading.

Name .... Section .... Date............

*Record your rate here:*_____
Average rate for freshmen on Chapter 12: 415 wpm.

application exercise: chapter 12

Enriching Your Vocabulary ...

A good foundation for vocabulary development can be built upon the bedrock of word analysis. Analyze a word into its component parts, and you break it into prefix, root, and suffix. There are nine common prefixes and fourteen common roots that, in their various combinations, are said to provide up to 100,000 words in an unabridged dictionary. Building from the familiar, we look at seven of those roots here:

capere (cept, cap, cip, capt) take, seize   *potere* (port, portat) carry
tenere (tain, ten, tin) hold, have   *graphein* (graph, gropho) write
mittere (met, mitt, miss) send   *logy* study of
ferre (fer) offer

Now look at the nine most common prefixes. By putting these beginnings of words on different roots, you can make hundreds of thousands of words. Because the nine listed here form the prefixes of the vast majority of prefixed words—some say these prefixes are used 90 per cent of the time in prefixed words, while 50 or more others are used the remaining 10 per cent of the time— it will pay to memorize them. If you have the nine prefixes and the seven roots firmly in mind, you will have a solid foundation for vocabulary development. The nine most common prefixes are:

com, con (with)   *dis* (apart from)
in (in)   *ex* (out of)
re (back, again)   *de* (from, away)
ad, a (to, toward)   *in, en* (in)
un, in (not)

Know for Test

The following master list includes the vocabulary words that have been selected from all the application exercises in Reading Skills. Analyze the list to determine what you can learn about roots and prefixes. Underline the roots you find from the list of seven and draw a circle around the prefixes you find from the list of nine. Thus: astrology, confute.

MASTER VOCABULARY LIST

The words on the following list come from the three *Vocabulary in Context* exercises, which may be found on pages 18, 42, and 72. Investigate the prefixes and roots.

abyss	discourse	obscenity
acclaim	disparaged	ominous
accredited	disposition	paltry
affection	emendator	parochial
alma mater	entity	phenomenon
antiquity	ephemeral	piety
archaic	extract	primer
aristocracy	fold in	prudence
assumption	foppery	pruning
astrology	futility	purged
astronomy	hallow	pusillanimous
bibliomaniac	harried	reciprocal
breach	humor	reprehensible
boon	illiterate	restitution
broad	impediment	singular
cant	impetus	sloth
cipher	immortal	sordid
cohere	imperishableness	spontaneity
cohesion	incorrigible	subjective
commensurate	incursions	titular
confute	inevitably	transmuting
consciousness	irresistible	unalienable
consecrate	manikins	usurpation
copiousness	marshaling	vexed
coteries	mayhem	vistas
countenance	metabolism	vital
coveted	morbid	voracity
cream	mutually	vulgarity
creed	mythological	wit
degenerating	nomenclature	worthies
despotism	noxious	wrought out

Taking Notes

13

Particularly when you are studying, the taking of notes is a valuable means of increasing reading efficiency. To be sure, taking notes will slow down your reading speed; on the other hand, it will force you to read more carefully.

Books are fine things, but they are not so sacred as some people think them to be. The familiar childhood command, "Do not write in books!" is so thoroughly drilled into some people that they feel a twinge of guilt whenever they are tempted to write in the margin. Certainly we shouldn't write in books that do not belong to us, but for your own books the command should be forgotten. In fact, many people feel that a book becomes more valuable to them if they do write in it. Furthermore, if the notes that are written in a book are intelligent ones, other readers of the book will benefit as well.

A good way to begin is to underline key statements. Some readers find it a good practice to underline a certain type of key statement, for example, the central idea of a chapter or section in red, the subordinate ideas in blue, and significant illustrations in black. If there is too much that seems to need underlining, perhaps you will want to jot down in the margin a statement of your own, summarizing a particular paragraph or section. Again you might use different colored pencils to show different types of material.

When you use a multicolor system you can review the book easily and in several ways. You can flip through the pages glancing only at those passages in red to find the central ideas, or you can be more thorough in your review and note the blue-penciled subordinate ideas and perhaps, the black-penciled illustrative passages as well. People who use this method say it helps them see things clearly and quickly.

Notes in the margin, for example, a clear phrasing of a topic idea or a comment of your own reaction to what you've read, may also be valuable. If your reading brings up a question that the author fails to answer, jot it down in the proper place in a margin. When you come to evaluating the book, such questions will be very helpful.

John Erskine, from whose Honors Course at Columbia grew the Great Books program, has his own ideas on note-taking. He says, "A book which is worth reading at all is likely to be read more than once, and at each reading some idea or some statement makes such an impression that we wish to refer to it again. Some readers underline the page as they read, but I find that a page which I have underlined cannot give me so many fresh impressions as one which has no marks on it. If I come to a passage already marked up, I remember the thoughts and feelings which prompted those first markings, and I have them again, with no additions. But a clean page may always give me something new."

Erskine continues, "My habit is make my own index of a book as I read. I put down the number of the page and a word or two to identify the thought or the fact which I get from it. On a second or third reading I am likely to double or triple the size of this index. This is my substitute for underlining. Most of the books in my library are so indexed that I can find quickly the passage which from time to time I wish to look up."

If a book is not your own and you wish to take notes on it, here are some suggestions that may help you get started. Take a look at the notebooks of some good students you know. Chances are you will find that the statements they have jotted down form an orderly sequence of ideas. Read them and they make sense. If necessary, they can be put away for months and even years and still be used to recapture the significant facts and ideas of the book that was read. Good notes, in short, should form a permanent, usable record. Bad notes, on the other hand, "grow cold." They are the notes over which we puzzle and say, "I wonder what that meant; I suppose I knew when I wrote it."

Taking notes on the standard 3 x 5 inch or 4 x 6 inch cards has several advantages. It is usually desirable to take notes and arrange them according to subject headings rather than according to sources.

A standard procedure is to write the subject of the card, say, "Spanish Civil War," in the upper right-hand corner and the author and title of the book in the upper left-hand corner. When you do this you can file the cards by subject, author, or title. Don't be stingy with your cards; they will be most helpful to you if they represent fairly narrow divisions of your subject. Your aim should be to have cards that you can shuffle and arrange to suit a variety of purposes.

Note-taking, like reading, can be done more efficiently if you do it with a special purpose in mind. The form of your notes should also be adapted to suit your purpose. An outline, for example, will help you to keep in mind the main ideas of the book and will help you remember the relation of the ideas. On the other hand, a summary—in your own words—will be easier to read and perhaps a little more satisfactory for review. A good general rule is to quote the author only if he puts the statement in a memorable way or if you know in advance that you will have a special use for the quotation. In most cases those notes in which you summarize material in your own words will be most useful to you.

application exercise: chapter 13

Taking Notes Is Not Copying . . .

A good note-taker constantly fights against the impulse to copy the reading instead of taking notes on it. The idea is to remember what you have read; furthermore, in this day of the copy machine, it is not necessary to transfer blocks of material from a text to your notes. Use the machine if you need to copy pages. Note-taking, on the other hand, is an opportunity to think out material as you read and to restate it in your own words.

Make brief and condensed notes of the following:

1. Earnest Lacy was a Philadelphia playwright whose plays were produced in the 1890's.

2. Thornton Wilder's *Our Town* (1938) tells the intimate history of Grover's Corners. New Hampshire, during the first decade of the century.

3. The two Puccini operas that were adapted from American plays are *Madame Butterfly* and *The Girl of the Golden West*. They were produced in the first decade of the century.

4. Clark Mills is chiefly known as the sculptor of the first equestrian statue in America, *General Jackson* (1853). Congress paid him $32,000 for it.

5. Tecumseh was a Shawnee Indian chief who tried to persuade the government to accept the principle that all Indian lands were a common possession that could not be ceded by or purchased from individual tribes.

6. Zane Grey was a writer of Western novels whose more than 60 books sold more than 13 million copies. Although he died in 1939, his most popular novel, *Riders of the Purple Sage*, was written in 1912.

7. Virgil Thomson wrote the music for two of Gertrude Stein's plays, *Four Saints in Three Acts* (1934) and *The Mother of Us All* (1946).

8. Horace Mann, who was instrumental in improving common-school education in this country, came to Antioch College as president in 1853 after losing the election for governor of Massachusetts.

Making Your Own Index . . .

Below, make your own index of this book. Follow John Erskine's advice as cited in the chapter, and index those topics that interest you most. Suggestions: authors of books, book titles, humorous anecdotes.

Summarizing

14

In a previous chapter you read that Bacon said, "Some books are to be chewed and digested...." For the books that need to be chewed and digested, making a written summary is an effective means to the end.

if, in taking notes on your reading, you put them in summary form *and in your own words*, you will find your notes much more useful to you than if you merely put down an occasional idea that strikes you as important. Such note-taking lacks clarity and organization. Your aim should be to have notes that represent, in capsule form, what you have read, and for this the best method is to summarize.

Summarizing forces you to exact comprehension: to do it well you must understand the author's main ideas and their relation to one another; you must record the key points in a connected form; and you must choose an economical and exact method of expression.

The only way to learn summarizing is by practice. Take an article that interests you and write down the topic sentences of each paragraph. When you finish, read what you have written and you will probably find that you have a fair summary of the article. Now write in transitions, making the relationship between sentences as clear as you can. Eliminate any unnecessary words. Abbreviate long words where you can and leave out any short ones that do not add to the meaning. Many students develop a personal shorthand for indicating various standard words and logical relationships. It is quite common, for example, to use three dots (∴) for "therefore" and an equals sign when two things are equated.

Another help in summarizing is to examine closely the author's final statement. If his argument there seems clear, you may find it helpful to restate what he says in your own words and add to it whatever is needed to make it most meaningful to you. It is foolish to try to keep in mind all the facts and examples that he has used to prove his point. But it is also foolish to make the mistake of thinking you will remember them all when you reread your own summary later. Include enough of them to be able to reconstruct his line of thought when you review your notes. It is not enough simply to know his conclusion.

Sometimes you will read a whole paragraph or two that will not contain anything worth recording. At other times, almost every sentence will seem crucial to an understanding of the chapter or section you are reading. Although one hesitates to say so, there are students who are over-conscientious and get bogged down in unimportant details. Fearful lest they overlook anything, their notes become so detailed as to be self-defeating. With practice and patience you will learn to separate the wheat from the chaff with increasing skill.

The whole process of summarizing implies an ability to make decisions. You have to decide what the author's plan is, how he has organized his material, what his key ideas are, and what material he uses merely as example. You will not find the technique of summarizing easy at first because it *does* require so many decisions. But your efficiency in making summaries, as well as your general reading efficiency, will increase in proportion to the time and effort you spend on perfecting your note-taking technique.

Your final summary should reflect clearly and accurately what the author has said. An inaccurate summary may be worse than no summary at all. An effective method of testing the quality of your summary is to set it aside for a month or two and then reread it. If it still recalls the essential information for you and if it still seems to express the material in a clear and exact manner, you have done a good job. If it does not, make another attempt. This time you will do a better job. This method, incidentally, may well be applied to other types of writing. Many a young writer has been advised to lay his material aside for a while. If a piece of writing seems as good a year or two later as the day you finished it, you can begin to feel that it will stand the test of time. The same thing, of course, applies to what someone else has written and you have read. If you think a book you read several years ago was the best you have known, reread it. Don't be surprised if you find yourself sadly disappointed.

Good summaries serve many purposes. Everyone, from professional man to housewife, needs and uses them. The doctor may have to summarize a report of his findings in a particular case for a medical board. He will have to read the summaries of other doctors and summaries of the latest medical research in his field. A lawyer needs to prepare a summary, or brief, of his case before he presents it in court. His summary usually takes the form of a sentence outline, and many a lawyer's early career is hurt by his inability to present a clear and accurate brief. A junior executive may write a summary of a long report for the president of the company. An electrical engineer will summarize his findings to formulate his plans. A publisher asks his assistants to make summaries of those manuscripts that he considers worth publishing. A student prepares summaries for use in a term paper.

The summary is a convenient and useful tool that saves you time, helps you remember, and lets you see the whole argument at a glance. It should never be regarded as an adequate substitute for reading a book. Once you have read a book, however, a good summary should make it unnecessary for you to spend time reading the book again. Though it slows down your reading, it may leave you more time for reading in the long run.

Name .... Section .... Date............

*Record your rate here:*_____
Average rate for freshmen on Chapter 14: 450 wpm.

application exercise: chapter 14

Getting It Together . . .

1. Summarize in as few words as possible the following excerpts:

   a. From Henry David Thoreau's <u>Civil Disobedience</u>: "There will never be a really free and enlightened state until the state comes to recognize the individual as a higher and independent power, from which all its own power and authority are derived, and treats him accordingly. I please myself with imagining a state at last which can afford to be just to all men, and to treat the individual with respect as a neighbor; which even would not think it inconsistent with its own repose if a few were to live aloof from it, not meddling with it, nor embraced by it, who fulfilled all the duties of neighbors and fellow-men. A state which bore this kind of fruit, and suffered it to drop off as fast as it ripened, would prepare the way for a still more perfect and glorious state, which also I have imagined, but not yet anywhere seen."

   b. From Abraham Lincoln's <u>Gettysburg Address</u> (see application exercise for Chapter 19).

   c. From <u>The Declaration of Independence</u> (see application exercise for Chapter 19).

   d. From William Faulkner's <u>Nobel Prize Acceptance Speech</u> (see application exercise for Chapter 23).

2. To apply the skills mentioned in this chapter, summarize the chapter itself in exactly one hundred words. Because the chapter is about one thousand words long, your summary will reduce it to about one-tenth its present length.

Making a Weekly Schedule

Time	Mon.	Tues.	Wed.	Thurs.	Fri.	Sat.	Sun.
7-8							
8-9							
9-10							
10-11							
11-12							
12-1							
1-2							
2-3							
3-4							
4-5							
5-6							
6-7							
7-8							
8-9							
9-10							
10-11							
11-12							

Using the Library

15

Once you have been bitten by the reading bug, you will have an incurable malady. You might as well resign yourself and settle down to a diet of books for the rest of your life. The disease, which is characterized by a voracious reading appetite and an insatiable curiosity about the world of books, can be quite painless if you let it run its natural course and pacify your appetite by reading as often as possible.

Like many other diseases, it can be treated only partially by home remedies—magazines, newspapers, and the books you buy. To combat it successfully, you will have to visit the local library frequently.

Fortunately there are thousands of free libraries about the country, thanks to wise legislators and city fathers, and especially to Andrew Carnegie, who built about 20 per cent of our public libraries. The fact that everyone can use these libraries means that, as a whole, Americans have a greater opportunity to read than any other people in the world. Still, all is not as it should be.

Ask an Englishman what Americans are like. He is likely to tell you something like this: "Americans admire bigness and large numbers; they want more of everything; they want things to be stupendous and colossal; they revere the tallest buildings and are awed by huge automobile plants manufacturing thousands of cars a day. Much of the time they worship size for its own sake to the neglect of other important things. They have, for example, more libraries than any other country, but half the people never read a book." Certainly it is never pleasant to listen to someone criticizing our country, but it is difficult not to admit that, in this case at least, truth has been spoken.

It is difficult to believe, but the hard fact is that half the citizens of our country, where nearly everyone can read, do not read one book a year. An investigation of the use of public libraries showed that for a 3-year period, 48 per cent of the people of the United States did not read a book and 18 per cent read less than four. That means that about one hundred million Americans did no book reading, or very little during one of the most crucial periods in our history. The investigation also showed that over half of the people who didn't read books didn't read magazines either, and sixteen million did not even read the newspaper. This in a nation to which the world looks for enlightened leadership.

If we are to be leaders, we should be readers, although few would argue that all wisdom comes from books and that Americans, therefore, should all rush to their nearest library. Yet it is certainly true that most of our competent leaders are avid readers; to arrive at wise decisions they must be well informed, which means reading widely in many fields.

Most persons who read widely, who devour book after book in search of knowledge and its companion, wisdom, must know how to use the resources of the public library. Let us assume that you are interested in learning about a specific topic and trace your course through the reference system of a library.

The topic in which you are interested is, let us say, world government. You know a little about it, and that little has whetted your appetite. You want to learn more. Your first move, of course, will be to go to the card catalog. Each book in the library will be listed on three cards in this catalog—one for the subject, one for the author, and one for the title of the book. If you cannot remember, offhand, the author or title of a book on world government, you can start with the subject card. There, under the subject of "World Government," you will quite probably find enough books listed to keep you busy for some time. In small libraries you may have to hunt on the shelves for the books you have selected from the catalog. Once you learn the library's system of classification you will be able to do this very easily. In a large library you will simply write the number of the book on a slip of paper, hand it to the librarian at the "call desk," and wait until it is delivered to you.

If it happens, as it often does, that the books you read whet your appetite for still more, you will want to return to the library and investigate the magazines. It is not necessary to go rummaging through the back numbers of all the magazines you think might have material on the subject. Consult *The Reader's Guide to Periodical Literature*, an invaluable aid to your reading on just about any subject. In the various recent volumes of the guide, under the heading of "World Government," you will find the information you need—names of articles and the magazines in which they appear, dates of publication, and so on. *The Reader's Guide* is bound into large volumes annually, but it is also published monthly, so that you can find material in current magazines as well. Look for the names of magazines that are most likely to suit your purpose, working back through the volumes for a few years or so. *The Atlantic, Harper's, The Congressional Digest,* and *Vital Speeches,* for example, are good magazines to use if you are looking for a critical and reasoned analysis, whereas *Newsweek, TV Guide,* and the women's magazines such as *Redbook* are more likely to provide a popular treatment of the subject. Most libraries subscribe to these periodicals, and you should have little trouble locating them.

Whether it is magazines or books that you read, and whether the subject in which you are interested is world government, Verdi, or Bang's Disease, the library is waiting to serve you. Don't be one of the millions who are strangers to its riches.

Name . . . . Section . . . . Date . . . .

*Record your rate here:*_____
Average rate for freshmen on Chapter 15: 465 wpm.

application exercise: chapter 15

Listing References . . .

Here is a short list of reference works available in almost any library that are basic tools for the research worker. Mark an X in front of the ones you are familiar with and make it your business to find out about the others.

MAGAZINE INDEXES

Annual Magazine Subject-Index (1908 -). Indexes about 150 periodicals, some in special fields, especially history.

Essay and General Literature Index (1900 -). Subject and author index to published volumes of essays.

Industrial Arts Index (1913 -). Subject index to material in engineering, technical, and business periodicals, books, and pamphlets.

International Index to Periodicals (1907 -). Indexes about 300 periodicals from various countries; includes historical, literary, political, and scientific subjects.

Poole's Index to Periodical Literature. Articles from American Magazines, 1802-1906.

Public Affairs Information Service (1905 -). "Public Affairs" is liberally interpreted.

Readers' Guide to Periodical Literature (1907 -). Indexes about 200 American magazines by author and subject. It can give references up to the preceding month.

NEWSPAPER INDEXES

The New York Times Index (1914 -). Appears monthly. This index is particularly helpful because it gives the dates of events that were presumably covered in all papers of the same date.

REFERENCE WORKS—GENERAL

Encyclopaedia Britannica, there are yearbooks for this encyclopedia from 1938 to date.

Encyclopedia Americana, yearbooks 1923 to date.

Dictionary of American Biography, 1928-1936, 20 vols.

Dictionary of National Biography, 1885-1937, 63 vols. and supplements. Biographies of Englishmen.

Who's Who in America, biennially since 1899.

Who's Who, British, annually since 1849.

World Almanac and Book of Facts, 1868 to date.

REFERENCE WORKS—TOPICAL

Architecture: *A History of Architecture on the Comparative Method* (Fletcher), 17th ed., 1961.

Art: *Encyclopedia of World Art,* 1959-1968, 15 vols. *Encyclopedia of the Arts* (Read), 1966. *Lives of the Painters* (Canaday), 1969, 4 vols. *McGraw-Hill Dictionary of Art* (Myers), 1969, 5 vols.

Business: *Encyclopedia of Banking and Finance* (Munn), 6th ed., 1962.

Chemistry: *Encyclopedia of Chemistry* (Clark), 2nd ed., 1966. *Thorpe's Dictionary of Applied Chemistry* (Thorpe and Whitely), 4th ed., 1937-1956, 12 vols.

Education: *Encyclopedia of Educational Research* (Harris), 3rd ed., 1960. *The Encyclopedia of Education* (Deighton), 1971, 9 vols.

Government and Political Science: *Cyclopedia of American Government* (McLaughlin and Hart), 1914, 3 vols. *Political Science: A Bibliographic Guide to the Literature* (Harmon), 1965.

History: *An Encyclopedia of World History* (Langer), 4th ed., 1968.

Literature: *Dictionary of World Literature* (Shipley), rev. ed., 1966.

Music: *Grove's Dictionary of Music and Musicians* (Blom), 5th ed., 1954, 9 vols.; supplement, Vol. 10, 1961. *The International Cyclopedia of Music and Musicians* (Thompson, rev. Sabin), 9th ed., 1964. *Harvard Dictionary of Music* (Apel), 2nd ed., rev., 1969. *The Oxford Companion to Music* (Scholes), 10th ed., 1970.

Philosophy: *The Encyclopedia of Philosophy* (Edwards), 1967, 8 vols.

Psychology: *Encyclopedia of Psychology* (Harriman), 1946. *A Dictionary of Psychology* (Drever), rev. ed., 1964.

Quotations: *Familiar Quotations* (Bartlett), 14th ed., 1968 *Dictionary of Quotations* (Evans), 1968. *The Oxford Dictionary of Quotations,* 2nd ed., 1953.

Religion: *New Catholic Encyclopedia,* 1967, 15 vols. and index. *Universal Jewish Encyclopedia,* 1939-1944, 10 vols. *Encyclopedia of Religion and Ethics* (Hastings), 1908-1927, 12 vols. and index. *New Schaff-Herzog Encyclopedia of Religious Knowledge* (Jackson), 1908-1912, 12 vols. and index; reprinted 1949-1950, 13 vols. *Twentieth Century Encyclopedia of Religious Knowledge* (Loetscher), 1955, 2 vols., an extension of *New Schaff-Herzog Encyclopedia of Religious Knowledge. Dictionary of the Bible* (Hastings), rev. ed., 1963.

Science: *Dictionary of Scientific Terms* (Speel and Jaffe), 1965. *Harper Encyclopedia of Science* (Newman), rev. ed., 1967. *Hutchinson's Technical and Scientific Encyclopedia* (Tweney and Shirshov), 1935, 4 vols. *The New Space Encyclopedia,* 1969. *Van Nostrand's Scientific Encyclopedia,* 4th ed., 1968. *Dictionary of Scientific Biography* (Gillispie), 1970, 2 vols. *McGraw-Hill Encyclopedia of Science and Technology,* 3rd ed., 1971, 15 vols.

Social Sciences: *Encyclopedia of the Social Sciences* (Seligman and Johnson), 1930-1935, 15 vols. *International Encyclopedia of the Social Sciences* (Sills), 1967, 16 vols. and index.

Time for Reading

16

It takes a long, long time to become a physician: four years of medical school after four years of college, then two or three years of internship, and often, finally, two or three years as a resident doctor in a hospital. By then the physician is ready to *begin* his career. But even then his work of preparation is not finished. He still has to devote much time to perfecting his skills. He has to *live* his profession 24 hours a day. When and if he becomes successful, it is in large measure because he has been willing to devote *time*, that most precious of all commodities, to his work.

Your work in reading, though not in a class with medical training, is like it insofar at least as it demands a willingness on your part to devote time to it. "But," you say, "I have too much to do already." What you probably mean is not that you have too much to do, but rather that you have too little time in which to do it. Here, then, are two suggestions for finding more time to read: organize yourself, and improve your reading habits.

Do you know some successful people? Is there a one of them who is not well organized? Probably not. Successful people in business, government, or almost any field you can mention organize themselves efficiently and budget their time. They realize the value of time very acutely, and they value it as a miser does his money. Ask the best student you know which he thinks is more valuable to him in his present status, time or money. He will probably say time. Time is precious. You will agree, then, it is unwise to squander it. Not that you shouldn't use a reasonable amount for rest and relaxation, but don't spend much time reading comics or daydreaming about what you will do with your first million dollars. Allot your time, part of it to serious reading, and deal with your first million when you get it. If you feel that reading is really important to you, you must find or *take* the time you need for doing it.

There is no best time for reading. It is true that there are certain periods during the day when your energy is at low ebb. For most of us one of these periods comes an hour or two before the evening meal. However, the periods vary with individuals. The best time for you depends on the organization of your day. It is therefore important to know what that time is and to use it for your reading work.

Many students insist that they already know how their day is organized, and they say they are aware of their "most alert" periods, yet they simply cannot find enough time for reading. The only thing to do is to find out the facts. The application exercise for this chapter suggests that you make a record of your daily activities to find out just how your time is spent. Keeping a record is a simple matter if you are willing to be systematic and if you are curious about what happens to your time. After a week of keeping tabs you will know how you spend your time and can change your schedule if the facts warrant a change.

Now a word about improving your reading habits to find more time. If you read relatively simple fiction, like Kenneth Robert's *Northwest Passage,* at the average adult reading rate of approximately 250 to 300 words per minute, you now realize that you could read it quite as well, if not better, at twice that rate—with the right kind of effort. One high-school boy who worked hard to improve his reading habits read *Northwest Passage* at 1200 words per minute, with excellent comprehension. People have read over 2000 words per minute with the same excellent comprehension. True, they had become very skillful readers; but they were not superhuman. Also, they did not skip any of the material but read every line. Think of the amount of material *they* could cover while someone else was meandering along at, say, 300 words per minute. Almost seven times as much. Is it not obvious why time is not the problem for such a person that it may be to you?

These rapid readers did not develop their efficient reading skills overnight. They devoted time to the job and worked seriously at it. Happily, unlike the amount of time necessary to become a physician, the time to become a skillful reader can be counted in weeks. Many people have doubled their reading rates in four weeks without sacrifice of comprehension. For others it may take a little longer. But if you can double your reading rate in a month or two, is it not worth while in terms of both time and pleasure? To do this you should be willing to devote some time each day to your reading program. Set aside the time and devote it exclusively to improving your reading. Allow no "days off." If you do take a vacation from reading after the first week or two, you hazard the chance of slipping back where you started.

When you finish this chapter you will have completed the first part of this book, which covers most of the important reading skills you will need for your college assignments. You should, by then, have formed a solid foundation on which to begin a lifetime of skillful reading. If you have the will, you will find the time to read. This is the same will that you must exercise in replacing your old inefficient reading habits with new ones. Time and will power are what you need.

Work hard at your assigned task and practice your improved habits whenever you pick up a book, leaf through a magazine, or read the newspaper. You must keep practicing.

Name .... Section .... Date............

*Record your rate here:*_____
Average rate for freshmen on Chapter 16: 475 wpm.

application exercise: chapter 16

Timing Yourself by the Week . . .

Almost every time you turn a page in this book you are asked to time yourself, but this time you are asked to make a different kind of timing operation. First, though, read the paragraphs below.

When Benjamin Franklin was about twenty-five, he devised a plan for "arriving at moral perfection." As part of his plan he drew up a list of virtues, and among these was Order, about which he said: "Let all your things have their places; let each part of your business have its time." In his Autobiography Franklin explains how he made a daily chart of his activities so he could organize himself more effectively. He found, however, that once he had established an orderly schedule, it was not easy to stick to it. He commented on this difficulty as follows:

read carefully

Franklin the Incorrigible

"My scheme of ORDER gave me the most trouble; and I found that tho' it might be practicable where a man's business was such as to leave him the dispostion of his time..., it was not possible to be exactly observed by a master, who must mix with the world, and often receive people of business at their own hours. *Order*, too, with regard to places for things, papers, etc., I found extremely difficult to acquire. I had not been early accustomed to it, and, having an exceeding good memory, I was not so sensible of the inconvenience attending want of method. This article, therefore, cost me so much painful attention, and my faults in it vexed me so much, and I made so little progress in amendment, and had such frequent relapses, that I was almost ready to give up the attempt, and content myself with a faulty character in that respect, like the man who, in buying an ax of a smith, my neighbour, desired to have the whole of its surface as bright as the edge. The smith consented to grind it bright for him if he would turn the wheel; he turn'd, while the smith press'd the broad face of the ax hard and heavily on the stone, which made the turning of it very fatiguing. The man came every now and then from the wheel to see how the work went on, and at length would take his ax as it was, without farther grinding. 'No,' said the smith, 'turn on, turn on; we shall have it bright by-and-by; as yet, it is only speckled.' 'Yes,' says the man, *'but I think I like a speckled ax best.'* And I believe this may have been the case with many, who, having, for want of some such means as I employ'd, found the difficulty of obtaining good and breaking bad habits in other points of vice and virtue, have given up the struggle, and concluded that *'a speckled ax was best'*; for something, that pretended to be reason, was every now and then suggesting to me that such

65

extreme nicety as I exacted of myself might be a kind of foppery in morals, which, if it were known, would make me ridiculous; that a perfect character might be attended with the inconvenience of being envied and hated; and that a benevolent man should allow a few faults in himself, to keep his friends in countenance.

"In truth, I found myself incorrigible with respect to Order; and now I am grown old, and my memory bad, I feel very sensibly the want of it. But, on the whole, tho' I never arrived at the perfection I had been so ambitious of obtaining, but fell far short of it, yet I was, by the endeavour, a better and a happier man than I otherwise should have been if I had not attempted it."

Now check the chart of daily activities you made for your weekly schedule when you worked on Application Exercise 2. Revise it in the light of your experience to date.

1. Is it sufficiently flexible?
2. Do you review material before class?
3. Are you able to carry out a plan for recreational reading?
4. Are your free hours really free of study?
5. What revisions are possible in the light of new understanding about "hard" and "easy" courses?
6. In the light of your revised estimates is it possible to find time for a creative outlet such as recreational painting, singing, or writing?
7. If you are having difficulty sticking to your schedule, as did Benjamin Franklin, what do you believe is the chief cause of the difficulty? Is it the imperfection of the schedule? Were you too optimistic? Were you too ambitious?

Part II

THE EVALUATIVE READING SKILLS

The basic reading skills that were considered and practiced in the first sixteen chapters of this book provide only the foundation for a full reading program. You will want to expand your reading beyond the bounds of required study materials, as time permits, not only to delve into the classics but also to keep abreast of current topics and to become acquainted with contemporary poetry and drama. These last chapters will guide you in choosing your reading matter and in critically appreciating your choices from the wide range of possibilities.

Why Read?

17

The previous chapters have emphasized some of the basic skills that should help you master your college reading tasks more effectively. But what of reading of the less immediately useful kind, the kind James Russell Lowell had in mind when he spoke of reading that "admits us to the whole world of thought and fancy and imagination"? This question is too often left unanswered in our colleges. Yet it is this kind of reading that leaves the strongest mark on us. Lowell also said, "Few men learn the highest use of books. After lifelong study many a man discovers too late that to have had the philosopher's stone availed nothing without the philosopher to use it."

Some years ago when the author faced his first class of students in an introduction to literature course, he tried to impress them with the values of "nonutilitarian" reading, that is, the reading we do other than to get a good mark in class or to learn a fact that will prove useful. When he discussed what Bacon wrote about studies serving to delight and added that man does not live by bread alone, the blank look on the students' faces made him wonder if he should have chosen to be a bricklayer rather than a teacher of literature.

If the author were to face that class again these are the reasons he would give for "nonutilitarian" reading. First of all, we should read to experience. Perhaps we can't take a trip to Europe, but we can share this experience with an author who has. Not only does a book take us to countries we can't visit ourselves, it can take us into the most fascinating place in the world, a man's mind. What was Whittaker Chambers thinking about during the Alger Hiss trial? His book, *Witness,* tells us. What was in Winston Churchill's mind during the Nazi air raids on Britain? His book, *Our Finest Hour,* tells us. We can't experience what these men have felt, but we can share their feelings through reading.

We read to satisfy our curiosity about these and many other things. In all of history most of the great discoveries have been made by men and women who were driven not by the desire to be useful but merely by the desire to satisfy their curiosity. A noted scientist, Abraham Flexner, who was for many years director of the famous Institute for Advanced Studies at Princeton, claims that curiosity brought about most of the important scientific contributions. "Curiosity," he says, "which may or may not eventuate in something useful, is probably the outstanding characteristic of modern thinking. It is not new. It goes back to Galileo, Bacon, and to Sir Isaac Newton, and it must be absolutely unhampered. Institutions of learning should be devoted to the cultivation of curiosity and the less they are deflected by considerations of immediacy of application, the more likely they are to contribute not only to human welfare but to the equally important satisfaction of intellectual interest which may indeed be said to have become the ruling passion of intellectual life in modern times."

We should read, therefore, both to satisfy and develop our curiosity. Why, for example, do people act the way they do? What controls them? A psychology or sociology text will lend some insight into this problem, but more fascinating, perhaps, are books like Theodore Dreiser's *An American Tragedy* or Richard Wright's *Native Son.* Are you curious about the chances for happiness of a boy who lives in the slums? James T. Farrell's *Studs Lonigan* looks keenly at this question. Do you know the problems of a drug addict? Read Nelson Algren's *The Man With the Golden Arm.* Do you understand how tenant farmers feel when corporations take over their farms? Read John Steinbeck's *The Grapes of Wrath.* Books like these, which may seem "nonutilitarian," both develop and satisfy our curiosity. As Flexner says, don't be "deflected by considerations of immediacy of application."

Read to get out of a mental rut. Read, in other words, for some of the same reasons you go to the movies. You want a change from your regular routine. You want to forget your troubles. You want to become someone else by identifying yourself with this or that hero or heroine and by losing yourself in a story. In short, read "nonutilitarian" books for relief from the humdrum routine of life.

Another reason for such reading is to help ourselves face the future more intelligently. A student may see no "use" in reading George Orwell's *1984* or Aldous Huxley's *Brave New World,* for example, but both these books present striking pictures of what a regimented world would be. Is this useful reading? The answer is yes, in proportion to your interest in the future. Of what use was it to Thomas Jefferson, a plantation owner, to read John Locke's *Essay on Civil Government?* By rights he should have been reading the colonial equivalent of farm bulletins and labor-management pamphlets. Fortunately for America, his "nonutilitarian" reading proved very useful in framing the Declaration of Independence and the Bill of Rights.

Read for appreciation and understanding. The more you know about the game of baseball, the more you appreciate it. As you learn about catcher's signals, pick-off plays, the hit-and-run, and sacrifices, the game becomes more interesting. After you have watched a few major league games, you appreciate the skill of the players. Just so with reading. The more you read about the life of Lincoln, the more you appreciate what he gave American life. Familiarity with the details of human experience, whether about baseball, Lincoln's life, or Samoan marriage customs, increases our ability to understand and appreciate that experience.

These, then, are some reasons for "nonutilitarian" reading. The chapters that follow will help you to deal more effectively with this kind of reading.

*Record your rate here:*_____
Average rate for freshmen on Chapter 17: 490 wpm.

application exercise: chapter 17

Reading Your Palm . . .

1. What is your inner nature? You could check your horoscope, or read Tarot cards, or go to a fortune teller. More rationally, you could look inside your mind. How do you behave in making choices? Why do you make the choices you do?

Listed next are categories of books. Indicate those you like by checking the appropriate categories:

____adventure (action)

____detective (clever? hard-boiled?)

____horror (terror? fright?)

____occult (the inexplicable)

____religious

____historical (local? authentic?)

____romance (young love? historical?)

____romance (overcomes odds?)

____topical (urban? suburban?)

____school (early days? current?)

____sea stories

____army stories (navy? marines? air force?)

____animal stories

____science fiction (the future?)

____biographies (living? historical?)

____art history (drama? music? other arts?)

____famous authors (name the author)

____poetry (traditional? contemporary?)

____drama (traditional? contemporary?)

____photography (other hobbies?)

2. What do the categories mean to you? The answer probably lies in your reasons for reading. You may say, for example, "I like action, adventure...." Or, you may say, "I like well-developed characters, people I would recognize on the street." In other words, your answer may uncover more than the surface, and it may well lead to self-discovery. Look into your consciousness and answer for each category you checked.

3. How does knowledge of your reading categories lead to self-discovery?

Do books help you live vicariously?

Do you read to satisfy your curiosity about how things work?

Do you read to see why people act the way they do?

Do you read to find the beauty, grace, and power in the world of artistic endeavor?

Do you read to escape from pressures that build up?

Does your pattern of reading reveal the kind of person you are? Such self-discovery helps us see ourselves more clearly and often with renewed insight into our own behavior.

Richard Wright, often considered the leading Black writer in the U.S., confesses that his life was changed by reading. In Black Boy he tells of seeing an editorial saying that H.L. Mencken was a fool. This made him want to read Mencken's books, which he did, by borrowing a white man's library card. Then he turned to other books, Sinclair Lewis's Main Street and Babbitt. He says, "Reading grew into a passion ... [it] was like a drug, a dope ... the novels created moods in which I lived for days."

VOCABULARY IN CONTEXT III

These words have been selected from the **Application Exercises** for Chapters 11 through 24. Match the words with their definition by writing the number of each word next to its definition. *The answer key is on page 70.*

Words from Chapters 16 and 18

1. disposition
2. vexed
3. foppery
4. in countenance
5. incorrigible
6. pusillanimous
7. cant
8. piety
9. parochial
10. voracity
11. futility
12. purged

__mean, low
__limited in outlook
__released
__handling
__not able to change
__sense of hopless-
  ness
__in favor with
__appetite
__insincere statement
__overconcerned
  about appearance
__upset
__reverence for God

Words from Chapters 19 and 20

1. consecrate
2. hallow
3. unalienable
4. prudence
5. usurpation
6. despotism
7. obscenity
8. vulgarity
9. morbid
10. mayhem

__tyranny
__murder
__immodesty, in-
  decency
__declare sacred
__unwholesomely
  gloomy
__safe and sober way
__coarseness
__act of taking over
__to make holy
__cannot be separated

Words from Chapters 21, 22 and 23

1. brood
2. immortal
3. transmuting
4. imperishableness
5. noxious
6. incursions
7. disparaged
8. emendator
9. bibliomaniac
10. sordid
11. boon
12. creed
13. commensurate
14. acclaim
15. ephemeral
16. ominous
17. harried
18. degenerating
19. abyss

__spoiled
__never dying
__has an excessive
  love of books
__gulf
__poisonous
__threatening
__equal to
__momentary
__meditate
__inroads
__favor
__changing
__one who corrects
__making smaller
__belief
__cannot be de-
  stroyed
__honor
__reproached
__bothered

Critical and Creative Reading

In order to be a skillful reader you need more than the right habits of moving your eyes across a page. You need to be able to think actively and creatively. This seems very obvious. Somewhat less obvious is the fact that the thinking we do while we read is concerned not merely with understanding but also with evaluating.

Every reader worth his salt is a critic, whether he knows it or not. He evaluates literature in the light of certain standards of taste that he sets up or that are established by custom. Is it important to read critically? To answer this question you need only ask if it is important for us to make sane judgments. As a citizen in a democracy, you know there is but one answer to this question. We all know the importance of reading critically under our type of government, the strength of which ultimately depends on the wisdom of the individual voter.

How can we qualify as competent critical readers? First of all, we need to establish a reasonably broad cultural background. The background of the true critical expert is broad indeed, much broader than we can, perhaps, ever hope to make our own. He has read many of the books the world considers great and feels justified in deciding, both for himself and for others, what is great and what is not. Competent critics are men like Matthew Arnold, John Ruskin, and in our own time, someone like Brooks Atkinson. Perhaps you have sometimes said to yourself, "Why must I accept the opinion of men such as these?" The answer is that often you have little choice. You accept the opinion of the traveler when he says Paris is wonderful because you have not been there and he has. Only when you visit the city yourself can you appraise his opinion and form your own. Only when you have read the great works of literature can you share in the determining of critical opinion about them.

It is far more difficult for most people to visit Paris than to read, say, the *Canterbury Tales, Tom Jones,* or *The Odyssey.* But even this, you say, is a long hard row to hoe. Certainly it is. The ground is fertile, however, and the work pleasant. And the result can bring you the greatest satisfaction in the world.

How to begin being a critical reader? Well, as we just finished saying, you need to establish a reasonably broad cultural background by reading widely. Yet, if in your own past experience you can find an illustration for a broad generalization that you have read, you have already begun the process of critical reading. The G.I. who finds himself sharing an experience with the soldier Prewitt in *From Here To Eternity* can do this. He reads that Prewitt was exhausted almost beyond the bounds of physical endurance, not by combat duty but by a drill sergeant who ran him ragged. The G.I. can fill in the details of the drill sergeant's tactics without any trouble. He merely remembers his own experience with drill sergeants, and he supplies all the illustrations he needs to support the generalization that Prewitt was tired. When he does this he is reading critically. Or if, also on the basis of your experience, you take exception to an author's point of view, you are reading critically. If you are reading a persuasive article and recognize the emotional basis of the writer's appeal, you are a critical reader. To some extent you are doing these things already—the more the better.

As a critical reader you will begin to feel that the printed page is not sacred. Authors are human. They make mistakes, they exaggerate, they overgeneralize just like the rest of us. Not to recognize this fact and to swallow all they have to say without even attempting to chew on it is to invite a bad case of indigestion. Too many people are inclined to say, "It must be so because the book says so." What nonsense! Test all books in the light of your experience and what you have read. Don't hesitate to play the role of the thoughtful critic.

On the other hand, do not make the mistake of discarding all that an author says just because you do not agree with this or that particular statement. Be critical of yourself as well as of the writer. Perhaps he is right and you are wrong. Re-examine what he says. Perhaps he didn't say what you thought he said. Are you sure you know what he means? In a particularly difficult passage it may pay to test each phrase, or even each key word independently. Examine them in every possible light; then make your final evaluation of them as they stand in the context.

A good reader is not only a critic; he is also a creator. His tool of creation is the same as the author's—his imagination. Using it, the good reader recreates the author's thought. Consider Shakespeare's *Hamlet* for example. An active, imaginative, and creative reading of the play should bring the reader a feeling of deep satisfaction, because he will begin to share in Shakespeare's imagination when he grasps the play through his own. The actor who portrays Hamlet on the stage must go even further. When his whole mind is pervaded by the imagination of Shakespeare, his response to the playwright's lines will be creative indeed. He reads and reads until, steeped in the verses, the word groupings come as naturally to him as if they were his own.

Creative and critical reading is the supreme test of a skillful reader. It requires every reading skill plus plenty of intellect, and it demands that he use the store of experience he has gained both from everyday life and from the printed page. Above all, it requires an inquiring mind and an ability to respond creatively.

application exercise: chapter 18

Speaking Critically . . .

1. Brooks Atkinson, the drama critic for the <u>New York Times</u>, has explained very clearly what he thinks the function of the critic and of criticism ought to be. The following is a selection from his "Credo of a Critic." Read it carefully; then do the exercise that follows.

The Most Profound Question

"On principle I do not subscribe to the pusillanimous notion that some people know what is good in art and others do not. There are no final authorities—least of all those who come to regard themselves as such. For there are no absolute standards in art save the ultimate one that cannot be defined because, like God, it goes deeper than articulate human experience. But some opinions are more valid than others. I respect the opinions of interesting people who bring to the appreciation of art the same sanity, vigor, and independence that they apply to their personal lives. Some people are more alive than others and what they think is accordingly vital and illuminating.

"As the years go by I have less and less respect for tradition, which I suspect is full of cant. From one generation to another we carry over a lot of piety about the good and the beautiful and it clutters up our spiritual world. Our mental furniture always needs a good rearranging, clearing out, and dusting. Traditional opinions are hardly worth the labor of writing. The only opinions that are valid come from people who are not parochial but touch life in many places, know many fields, have wide interests, and manage somehow to retain a freshness of impression. In fact, there should be a large dash of the amateur in criticism. For the amateur is a man of enthusiasm who has not settled down and is not habit-bound.

"Although I do not rank criticism among the highest forms of literary work, I am far from regarding it as negligible. On the contrary, it has always interested me very much. I have always had a great voracity for opinions. They are the electricity of the mind. 'What do you think?' Is there a more profoundly social question than that? It assumes that we are all living together and have within ourselves the power to sort things out and create a civilization. No community is wholly alive that is not interested in art, which is the mirror of human beings, and that does not have vigorous opinions about art and artists. If it feels deeply about these things, it also has enough energy to look after other public affairs. In short, it has a future.

"It is the function of the critic to pitch into the intellectual life of the community and express his opinion with force and clarity. What he knows about the technique of his field is valuable, but not half so valuable as his interests in and knowledge of the life of human beings."

Brooks Atkinson

Comment on the following statement: "The trouble with Brooks Atkinson's 'Credo' is that, in a world designed by him, all men would be critics, and there would be less emphasis on what the world really needs, creative activity."

Critical Limits

2. In his Poetics, Aristotle explains that the object of art is to show men in action. He says that when dramatic action (the theater) reveals the fullness and futility of life (as opposed to comic situations), certain limits make it work: (1) the action takes place within a single revolution of the sun; (2) the emotions of pity and fear, excited by the plot, are purged or released; (3) situations in the plot are reversed or the unknown is recognized; (4) the hero falls from high estate to low through a flaw in his character (pride); and (5) the unraveling of the plot comes through the action of the plot itself, not by some artificial device (God from the machine).

Use Aristotle's "limits" to criticize a play or movie you have seen recently.

One Pre-established Design

3. In his review of Hawthorne's Twice-Told Tales, Edgar Allan Poe reveals the essence of short-story writing. He says a tale should have a single effect and all the incidents of the story should be imagined and combined to produce this preconceived effect: "there should be no word written, of which the tendency . . . is not to the one pre-established design." "The true critic," Poe says, "will but demand that the design intended be accomplished, to the fullest extent, by the means most advantageously applicable."

Use Poe's ideas to criticize a story you have read recently.

The Why and How
of Analyzing

19

Many people object to analyzing a poem or a story. They feel that, somehow or other, a dissection will destroy its beauty or its mood. They don't like to take a thing apart for fear it might never become a "living" whole again. Even if one explains that the instrument of dissection is their own mind and that a piece of literature will become much more alive and meaningful when they learn to see the relation of its parts to the whole, they still react violently against the idea.

But there is no other way to find the essential qualities of a good work of art than by examining it, so to speak, with X-ray eyes. Before the X-ray was invented, physicians had to guess about the arrangement of the parts of a living organism. They had to rely on an imperfect method. But when they could examine with the X-ray, the preciseness of their knowledge increased enormously. And note this: Their subject remained alive while they were investigating. They did not worry about destroying the beauty of the organism, just as the patient did not complain about having his inner self invaded. The X-ray was universally acclaimed as a useful tool to greater knowledge and understanding, and there was less need for intuitive medical analysis.

Just so can logical analysis help the reader of a book. Emily Dickinson can say that she knows good poetry intuitively because, "I feel physically as if the top of my head were taken off"; but to understand and appreciate a book, a reader should attempt to discover what its parts are, how they relate to each other, and what binds them into one unified whole. As we have already said, he does not endanger the living character of a book. Rather, a careful analysis of a book is the best way to bring it to life, to make it become vital and beautiful. Alexander Pope once said that when you dissect an insect in order to determine what makes it live, you lose life at the moment you detect it. But, as Pope would be the first to remind us, a book is not an insect. The moment you detect what makes a book live, it becomes forever yet more alive. And you detect what makes it live by dissecting it.

A very poor book may be compared to an amoeba, the simplest form of animal life. It has little structure, being merely a mass of relatively unrelated parts flowing unpredictably and without pattern. A very good book, on the other hand, may be compared to *homo sapiens,* the most complex form of animal life. It has a very complete and thoroughly unified structure; the parts are closely related and move in definite and determinable ways toward a goal.

Your job as a reader of a good book is to determine its structure, the relationship of its parts, and the way it moves toward its goal. You go about determining these things by asking an imaginary question of the author. You ask what his book is about; that is, what is its main point. Back of this question is your thinking about the book's unity. You are looking for the theme about which the book moves. Once you think you have determined the main point, try stating it in as few words as possible. Even in such an immense novel as *Gone With the Wind* the theme can be stated in a few simple and familiar words: girl meets boy; girl gets boy; girl loses boy. You cannot always reduce a book to such simple terms, but when you do thus strip it to its barest essentials, you begin to find out what makes it live. In *Gone With the Wind*, for example, you find that the essence of part one is: girl meets boy; part two: girl gets boy; and part three: girl loses boy. The Civil War acts as an effective backdrop for this ancient story formula.

Next you should be able to indicate what the parts of the book are, as we have shown, in very general terms, for *Gone With the Wind*. On a simple level it works like this. When you go to a play you may notice that each act is, in a sense, a play in itself. Consider Arthur Miller's two-act play, *Death of a Salesman*, as an example. In Act One, Willy Loman's life is revealed to the audience. His dreams and ambitions have been devoted to a false criterion of success, namely to be well liked and to make money at the expense of everything else. Willy tells his sons, "The man who makes an appearance in the business world, the man who creates personal interest, is the man who gets ahead. Be liked and you will never want." At the end of the act the audience senses quite deeply the tragedy of Willy's existence. The act is a complete unit, for it shows Willy's fall from high estate to low, and it leaves unresolved only the means of his final descent to death. Act Two heightens the tragedy when the sons revert hopelessly to the same false standards that led to Willy's failure. This act is a complete unit also, and with a few changes it might stand alone as a well-integrated play. Alone, each act would present a fascinating study; together they form a deeply moving tragedy, each act contributing its share to our understanding of a man who destroys himself.

The principle of analyzing parts is the same for a novel or a poem. In a novel you consider the chapters; in a poem, the stanzas or cantos. These divisions make up the apparent structure of a work as the author saw it. You may see it another way, but the important thing is this: the good reader sees the whole, the parts, and the relationship of the parts.

application exercise: chapter 19

Analyzing a Sample . . .

Read the short analysis of Lincoln's "Gettysburg Address," which shows how some of the principles of analyzing may be applied. When you have finished, analyze the Declaration of Independence.

The Gettysburg Address

Fourscore and seven years ago our fathers brought forth on this continent a new nation, conceived in liberty, and dedicated to the proposition that all men are created equal.

Now we are engaged in a great civil war, testing whether that nation, or any nation so conceived and so dedicated, can long endure. We are met on a great battlefield of that war. We have come to dedicate a portion of that field as a final resting place for those who here gave their lives that that nation might live. It is altogether fitting and proper that we should do this.

But, in a larger sense, we cannot dedicate—we cannot consecrate—we cannot hallow—this ground. The brave men, living and dead, who struggled here, have consecrated it far above our poor power to add or detract. The world will little note nor long remember what we say here, but it can never forget what they did here. It is for us, the living, rather, to be dedicated here to the unfinished work which they who fought here have thus far so nobly advanced. It is rather for us to be here dedicated to the great task remaining before us—that from these honored dead we take increased devotion to that cause for which they gave their last full measure of devotion; that we here highly resolve that these dead shall not have died in vain; that this nation, under God, shall have a new birth of freedom; and that government of the people, by the people, for the people, shall not perish from the earth.

ANALYSIS

Purpose

The beginning and end of the speech indicate that Lincoln was attempting to define the American democratic philosophy. The middle of the speech and the title indicate that he was dedicating a cemetery. This much the speech itself tells us. The historical background of the speech reveals that Lincoln, who had been accused of making jokes about the dead a year before, wanted the people to know his true character. Thus, the emphasis on dignity and sincerity. It also reveals that pressure was put on Lincoln to speak out for democracy, popular government, and the masses.

79

Figurative language links the time order of Lincoln's speech to the basic cycle of life: "our fathers brought forth a new nation, conceived in liberty" (birth); "and dedicated" (baptism); "long endure" (life); "final resting place" (death); and "new birth of freedom" (rebirth). The biblical tone of the speech ("Fourscore and seven," "our fathers," "dedicated," "consecrate," and "hallow") makes it appealing to those whose feelings stem from Christianity.

Organization
The logical, chronological, and spatial organization of the speech is as follows: Logical — (1) these ceremonies are appropriate, but (2) the living cannot dedicate this ground; instead (3) the living should themselves be dedicated; Chronological — from past to present to future; Spatial — the subject is narrowed from continent to nation to battlefield and then enlarged from this nation to, finally, the world.

Now analyze the following selection from The Declaration of Independence. First reduce it to five or six sentences and show how one part is related to another, then comment on the purpose and on the appropriateness of the language.

The Declaration of Independence

When, in the course of human events, it becomes necessary for one people to dissolve the political bands which have connected them with another, and to assume among the powers of the earth, the separate and equal station to which the Laws of Nature and of Nature's God entitle them, a decent respect to the opinions of mankind requires that they should declare the causes which impel them to the separation.

We hold these truths to be self-evident, that all men are created equal, that they are endowed by their Creator with certain unalienable rights, that among these are Life, Liberty and the pursuit of Happiness. That to secure these rights, governments are instituted among men, deriving their just powers from the consent of the governed. That whenever any form of government becomes destructive of these ends, it is the right of the people to alter or to abolish it, and to institute new government, laying its foundation on such principles and organizing its powers in such form, as to them shall seem most likely to effect their safety and happiness. Prudence, indeed, will dictate that governments long established should not be changed for light and transient causes; and accordingly all experience hath shewn, that mankind are more disposed to suffer, while evils are sufferable, than to right themselves by abolishing the forms to which they are accustomed. But when a long train of abuses and usurpations, pursuing invariably the same object, evidence a design to reduce them under absolute despotism, it is their right, it is their duty, to throw off such government, and to provide new guards for their future security. Such has been the patient sufferance of these colonies; and such is now the necessity which constrains them to alter their former systems of government. The history of the present king of Great Britain is a history of repeated injuries and usurpations, all having in direct object the establishment of an absolute tyranny over these states. To prove this, let facts be submitted to a candid world....

Standards of Judgment

20

If you are enthusiastic about sports you recognize immediately a poor performance by an athlete or by a team. You know from having watched many sports events that a certain standard of performance is expected. You also know that when an athlete, for example, a baseball player, enters the professional ranks, he has to meet the highest standards. If he doesn't, he quickly finds himself ranked with the amateurs.

A man who publishes a novel has also entered the professional ranks, and he, too, must meet the highest standards. If he doesn't, he too, quickly finds himself ranked with the amateurs.

We have all been in groups where athletics or novels are being discussed, and we know that in such groups there are always those who sound off merely for the sake of hearing their own voices. They glean some items of information or opinion from someone who, they think, is really "in the know." Then they spring this "knowledge" at the first opportunity. They work it into the conversation and hope that we will regard them as authorities. Most of the time, however, we are not fooled—at least not for long.

In contrast to the false authority is the man who really knows. His remarks carry the weight of wide and long experience. In the case of athletics, such a man is either one who has been a player himself or one who has carefully observed a large number of sports events. He is believed because he has had the opportunity to compare many performances. He knows when an athletic performance is better than average, because he knows what excellence is. The same is true of the man who knows novels. His opinion is respected either because he is a novelist himself or because he has read, intelligently, a great many novels. His remarks carry conviction because he bases them on experience and intimate acquaintance with the novelist's art. As they say at the race track, "He talks like a man with a tip straight from the horse's mouth."

What are some of the standards by which we measure a book? First of all, there is the matter of legibility. Perhaps this seems almost too obvious, but it certainly does influence our judgment. To judge a book you must be able to read it easily. The size of type, color of page and print, and size of margins should not be a hindrance to reading. Next, there is the matter of language, a standard that can vary from the simple to the extremely complex. For most of us, the book must be written in a language we can read, not Sanscrit or Egyptian or Zulu, but English. However, we know all too well that a book can be written in English and still not be easily understood. Our judgment for such a book becomes one of style; we consider the author's manner of expression. In reading to gain knowledge, it is sufficient if the author imparts information clearly. When we read a book as a work of art, we look for clarity of expression, but for something more, too. It is at this point of "something more" that a consideration of standards progresses from the merely useful to the aesthetic—to the consideration of artistic beauty.

What is the "something more" we search for in the writing of a novel or short story? One thing we are especially conscious of is the language used. Not only must it be on a mature level (most adults resent having to read *Tom Sawyer* adapted for fourth-grade use), but it must also be *appropriate* to the design of the story. The matter was admirably stated by Edgar Allan Poe, who said, "In the whole composition, there should be no word written, of which the tendency, direct or indirect, is not to the one pre-established design." But employing the standard of language that Poe sets up means determining the author's purpose, what Poe calls "the one pre-established design." There is a style for sarcasm, for irony, for mystery, for horror, and so on. Let one example from the last paragraph of Poe's "The Fall of the House of Usher" serve to show what he considered to be an appropriate style for horror. "From that chamber, and from that mansion, I fled aghast. The storm was still abroad in all its wrath as I found myself crossing the old causeway. Suddenly there shot along the path a wild light, and I turned to see whence a gleam so unusual could have issued; for the vast house and its shadows were alone behind me. The radiance was that of the full, setting and blood-red moon." There is an appropriate style for every purpose, and it is up to the reader to judge the style in the light of whatever the purpose happens to be.

There are still other standards by which literature should be judged. Most of them are concerned with what we shall call, for want of a better phrase, enrichment of life. The critical reader must ask himself: "Does this book help me understand human nature a little better?" This question is one that will be accompanied by others: "Is this author's point of view about human nature a reasonable one? Is it possible that, given these characters and this plot, people would act like this? Is the plot plausible? Are the characters true to life?" The questions, of course, will depend on the work at hand, but they all lead to our asking: "Does this author really have anything to say to me, and shall I change or enlarge my view of life because of what he says?"

Everyone sets up standards of his own by which he judges other people's views of life. No one else can decide your standards. In some degree, therefore, a work of literature is good or bad or something between good and bad, as *you* see it.

Name .... Section ....Date............

Record your rate here:_____
Average rate for freshmen on Chapter 20: over 500 wpm.

application exercise: chapter 20

Looking for the Humor . . .

Attempts to set up standards of judgment have been made in various areas of our culture. Journalists have a code by which they judge a newspaper. There is a code for the making of motion pictures in this country. A beginning toward a code has been made in the multimillion-dollar comic book industry, but for a long time still the only effective code for comic books will be the public's code reflected in its refusal to buy inferior products. Pressure exerted by exasperated parents is forcing improvements in television programming for children at least.

Listed below are the standards set up by the Committee on Evaluation of Comic Books. The committee warns that they are intended to serve primarily as guides and check-points in the evaluation of comic books, rather than as complete standards which must in all cases be applied literally and rigidly. They should, warns the committee, be used by the reviewer in the light of his best judgment regarding good taste, the intent and spirit of the story, and the context of the individual frames of the story.

Criteria for Evaluating Comic Books

I. Cultural Area
  No Objection:
    1. Good art work, printing, and color arrangement
    2. Good diction
    3. The over-all effect pleasing
    4. Any situation that does not offend good taste from the viewpoint of art or mechanics
  Some Objection:
    1. Poor art work, printing, and color arrangement
    2. Mechanical set-up injurious to children's eyes; print too small; art work crowded
    3. Poor grammar and underworld slang
    4. Undermining in any way traditional American folkways
  Objectionable:
    1. Propaganda against or belittling traditional American institutions
    2. Obscenity, vulgarity, profanity, or the language of the underworld
    3. Prejudice against class, race, creed, or nationality
    4. Divorce treated humorously or as glamorous
    5. Sympathy with crime and the criminal as against law and justice
    6. Criminals and criminal acts made attractive
  Very Objectionable:
    1. An exaggerated degree of any of the above-mentioned acts or scenes
II. Moral Area
  No Objection:
    1. An uplifting plot
    2. Wholesome characters

3. Characters dressed properly for the situation
4. If crime, when it enters the plot, is incidental
5. Any situation that does not compromise good morals

Some Objection:
1. Criminal acts or moral violation even if given legal punishment
2. The presence of criminals, even if they are shown as not enjoying their crimes

Objectionable:
1. Women as gun molls, criminals, and the wielders of weapons
2. Any situation having a sexy implication
3. Persons dressed indecently or unduly exposed
4. Crime stories, even if they purport to show that crime does not pay
5. Situations that glamorize criminals
6. The details or methods of crime, especially if enacted by children
7. Thwarted justice
8. Law enforcement official portrayed as stupid or ineffective

Very Objectionable:
1. An exaggerated degree of any of the above-mentioned acts or scenes

III. Morbid Emotionality
No Objection:
1. Any situation that does not arouse morbid emotionality in children

Some Objection:
1. Overrealistic portrayal of death of villains
2. Grotesque, fantastic, unnatural creatures
3. Imminent death of a hero or heroine

Objectionable:
1. The kidnaping of women or children, or the implication of it
2. Characters shown bleeding, particularly from the face or mouth
3. The use of chains, whips, or other cruel devices
4. The picturization of dead bodies
5. Stories and pictures that tend to upset children
6. Anything having a sadistic implication
7. Portrayal of mayhem, acts of assault, or murder
8. People being attacked or injured by animals or reptiles

Very Objectionable:
1. An exaggerated degree of any of the above mentioned acts or scenes

A. Using these criteria, evaluate a number of comic books and list those you would recommend to others
B. Evaluate the criteria (written in 1952). Would you recommend any changes? In your opinion do such codes work?

Reading Great Literature

21

What makes a book great? Mark Twain is supposed to have said that great books were those everybody recommends and no one reads. Each man has his own list of great books, and it would be foolish to insist on uniformity of opinion, but it is *not* foolish to try to express our ideas of what makes a book great. Doing so helps sharpen critical perception and makes us read with a keener appreciation.

Great literature is generally an original communication, a contribution to some unsolved problem of human life. Generally, too, it has a notable style derived from the care with which the author has fashioned his work. It goes without saying that competent reading of great books requires a real effort of attention. In order to get the most out of such a book you must give your best to it.

James Russell Lowell emphasizes this point when he says, "Among books, certainly, there is much variety of company, ranging from the best to the worst, from Plato to Zola, and the first lesson in reading well is that which teaches us to distinguish between literature and merely printed matter. The choice lies wholly with ourselves. Every book we read may be made a round in the ever-lengthening ladder by which we climb to knowledge and to that temperance and serenity of mind which, as it is the ripest fruit of Wisdom, is also the sweetest. But this can only be if we read such books as make us think, and read them in such a way as helps them to do so, that is, by endeavoring to judge them, and thus to make them an exercise rather than a relaxation of the mind."

In his *Sesame and Lilies*, John Ruskin also speaks eloquently on the subject. "The author," he remarks, "has something to say which he perceives to be true and useful, or helpfully beautiful. So far as he knows, no one has yet said it; so far as he knows, no one else can say it. He is bound to say it, clearly and melodiously if he may; clearly at all events. In the sum of his life he finds this to be the thing, or group of things, manifest to him;—this, the piece of true knowledge, or sight, which his share of sunshine and earth has permitted him to seize. He would fain set it down forever; engrave it on rock, if he could, saying, 'This is the best of me: for the rest, I ate and drank, and slept, loved, and hated, like another; my life was as the vapour, and is not; but this I saw and knew; This, if anything of mine, is worth your memory.' That is his 'writing'; it is, in his small human way, and with whatever degree of true inspiration is in him, his inscription, or scripture. That is a 'Book'."

As great literature is a record of the best that man has thought and said, it certainly deserves the right kind of reading. Here are a few suggestions about the reading of great literature. Read first for sheer enjoyment. Since the great literary classics are worth more than one perusal, read the first time as an adventurer exploring a new world. When you finish, set the book aside for a few days. Think about it occasionally. Let it form its impression on your mind. Then after a week or so—or a month if need be—go back to it. This time read it more carefully. If it is a work of fiction, start looking for the fine points of characterization and plot. Read to see what makes the work great.

The idea that great literature depends a good deal on the reader as well as the writer has often been expressed. Emerson was thinking about the reader in his American Scholar Address over one hundred years ago when he spoke about poets and poetry. He emphasized the fact that the reader must bring an active mind to reading. No wise man, he contended, would read and accept blindly. Reading great literature is an activity that requires constant alertness. He said, "Great and heroic men have existed, who had almost no other information than by the printed page. I would say that it needs a strong head to bear that diet. One must be an inventor to read well. There is creative reading as well as creative writing. When the mind is braced by labor and invention, the page of whatever book we read becomes luminous with manifold allusion. Every sentence is doubly significant, and the sense of our author is as broad as the world."

Not many works of American literature are written with a "sense as broad as the world," but there are some American novels that critics agree deserve to be read as classics. They are Nathaniel Hawthorne's *The Scarlet Letter*, Herman Melville's *Moby Dick*, Mark Twain's *Huckleberry Finn*, and in our own times, John Dos Passos' *U.S.A.* and Sinclair Lewis' *Babbitt*. Each can be read and reread and read again. Every time you enter the magic realm of one of these books, you will find something new, something that you somehow missed before. They are a joy to read.

Emerson, speaking of the keen delight of great literature, said, "It is remarkable the pleasure we derive from the best books. They impress us with the conviction that one nature wrote and the same reads. There is some awe mixed with the joy of our surprise, when this poet, who lived in some past world, says that which lies close to my own soul, that which I also had well nigh thought and said."

Remember that the authors of books we now consider great did not write them merely for scholars. For the most part they wrote with great clarity for everyone who could read. Great books, then, are yours; they were not meant to be the possession of the few. Bring them your best and they will give you endless pleasure.

*Record your rate here:*_____
Average rate for freshmen on Chapter 21: over 500 wpm.

application exercise: chapter 21

Listing Basic Books . . .

The following is a list of basic books that Thomas Craven and Norman Corwin would buy first if their personal libraries were somehow destroyed:

BE
FAMILIAR

Thomas Craven		Norman Corwin	
Burns	*Poems*	Marquis	*Archie and Mehitabel*
Fielding	*Tom Jones*	Steinbeck	*Grapes of Wrath*
Twain	*Huckleberry Finn*	Hersey	*The Wall*
Balzac	*Old Goriot*	Keats	*Poems*
Lewis	*Babbitt*	Whitman	*Leaves of Grass*
Keats	*Poems*	Swift	*Gulliver's Travels*
Whitman	*Leaves of Grass*	Franklin	*Autobiography*
Wells	*Outline of History*	Shakespeare	*Plays*
Swift	*Gulliver's Travels*	Rabelais	*Gargantua and Pantegruel*
Franklin	*Autobiography*	Paine	*Writings*
Hardy	*Tess of the D'Urbervilles*	Melville	*Moby Dick*
Hemingway	*Farewell to Arms*	Masters	*Spoon River Anthology*
Maugham	*Of Human Bondage*	Freud	*Writings*
Homer	*Iliad* and *Odyssesy*	Sandburg	*Abraham Lincoln*
Cervantes	*Don Quixote*		*The People, Yes*
Dickens	*David Copperfield*	Carroll	*Alice in Wonderland*
Dreiser	*An American Tragedy*	Wells	*Science of Life*
	Sister Carrie	Thoreau	*Walden*
O'Neill	*Plays*	Falstaff	*Reini Kugel*
Faulkner	*Collected Stories*	Shaw	*Plays*
Tolstoi	*Anna Karenina*	Wassermann	*The World's Illusion*
	War and Peace	B. Smith	*The Democratic Spirit*
		Evans	*Natural History of Nonsense*
		_____	*The Bible* ✓

Check those books on the list that you have read. Then list at least three of the basic books <u>you</u> would buy if your library were destroyed and tell why you think they are great books.

Read the following selection from Ralph Waldo Emerson's <u>The American Scholar</u> (1837) and be prepared to answer the analytical question, "Which book has made the strongest impact on me?" Any value to the question will lie in the specifics of your answer.

No Perfect Book

The theory of books is noble. The scholar of the first age received into him the world around; brooded thereon; gave it the new arrangement of his own mind, and uttered it again. It came into him life; it went out from him truth. It came to him short-lived actions; it went out from him immortal thoughts. It came to him business; it went from him poetry. It was dead fact; now, it is quick thought. It can stand, and it can go. It now endures, it now flies, it now inspires. Precisely in proportion to the depth of mind from which it issued, so high does it soar, so long does it sing.

Or, I might say, it depends on how far the process had gone, of transmuting life into truth. In proportion to the completeness of the distillation, so will the purity and imperishableness of the product be. But none is quite perfect. As no air-pump can by any means make a perfect vacuum, so neither can any artist entirely exclude the conventional, the local, the perishable from his book, or write a book of pure thought, that shall be as efficient, in all respects, to a remote posterity, as to contemporaries, or rather to the second age. Each age, it is found, must write its own books; or rather, each generation for the next succeeding. The books of an older period will not fit this.

Yet hence arises a grave mischief. The sacredness which attaches to the act of creation, the act of thought, is transferred to the record. The poet chanting was felt to be a divine man: henceforth the chant is divine also. The writer was a just and wise spirit: henceforward it is settled the book is perfect; as love of the hero corrupts into worship of his statue. Instantly the book becomes noxious: the guide is a tyrant. The sluggish and perverted mind of the multitude, slow to open to the incursions of Reason, having once so opened, having once received this book, stands upon it, and makes an outcry if it is disparaged. Colleges are built on it. Books are written on it by thinkers, not by Man Thinking; by men of talent, that is, who start wrong, who set out from accepted dogmas, not from their own sight of principles. Meek young men grow up in libraries, believing it their duty to accept the views which Cicero, which Locke, which Bacon, have given; forgetful that Cicero, Locke, and Bacon were only young men in libraries when they wrote these books.

Hence, instead of Man Thinking, we have the bookworm. Hence the book-learned class, who value books, as such; not as related to nature and the human constitution, but as making a sort of Third Estate with the world and the soul. Hence the restorers of readings, the emendators, the bibliomaniacs of all degrees.

Books are the best of things, well used; abused, among the worst. What is the right use? What is the one end which all means go to effect? They are for nothing but to inspire. I had better never see a book than to be warped by its attraction clean out of my own orbit, and made a satellite instead of a system. The one thing in the world, of value, is the active soul.

Reading Poetry

22

Point one: Poetry should usually be read aloud. With some modern exceptions, it was written to be read that way. Point two: Do not attempt to race through poetry in the same manner that you race through a light novel. The results will be discouraging if you do.

Poets are not like other writers. For one thing they constantly strive for economy of expression. Not one word is wasted; each one has its place in the pattern of a poem. For another thing, they are very careful to choose just the right words, words that bring an exact shade of meaning to the poem. The right word carefully selected and exquisitely placed, provides the poet's greatest challenge. In short, poets are word-conscious to an uncommon degree.

Not only are they conscious of word meanings, they are also highly sensitive to word sounds. This does not mean that a poet's words will be soft, sweet, and melodious at all times. Some very effective and powerful poems depend for their forcefulness on words that are almost brutally rude and strong. In Kenneth Fearing's "Dirge," for example, when he speaks of the death of a man he comments rather critically, "Zowie did he live and zowie did he die." The impact of that line, and of the whole poem for that matter, is tremendously increased if you read it aloud.

Poets, as you can see, expect you to *speak* and not simply read their lines. Obviously, you cannot read a poem aloud any faster than you can speak; slowness of reading is, in this instance, positively desirable. If you go too fast, you lose the flavor. Racing through good poetry is like gulping down a wine that was meant to be sipped, tasted, and appreciated. As with good wine, you should savor a poem. Give it a chance to provide its full measure of delight.

Besides words or sounds, you should consider the rhythm when you read a poem. To do this you do not have to keep time by imitating the fat, black bucks in Vachel Lindsay's poem, "The Congo," who "beat an empty barrel with the handle of a broom." But you should be aware of the rhythm and the subtle effect it has on the reader.

Something else that is important is the imagery or figurative language of a poem. Imagery gives enormous concentration to an idea and presents it in an economical way. It brings an idea to life, drives home a startling insight, makes a common thing take on an uncommon significance. Consider these lines from an Emily Dickinson poem. She complains that something dropped so low in her regard that she heard it fall to earth "and go to pieces on the stones/at bottom of my mind." Because imagery is so concentrated, it should be taken slowly and examined carefully. A great deal of the pleasure to be derived from reading poetry comes from an awareness of effective imagery.

Poets are fond of twisting an old idea around and presenting it in a new light. The idea is old, but what a difference in the expression. Giving voice to the idea that mere money-grubbing is not the means to a rich experience of life, Wordsworth wrote his memorable lines declaring, "The world is too much with us, late and soon,/ Getting and spending we lay waste our powers." Emerson echoed the idea when he wrote, "Things are in the saddle and ride mankind." The same idea, but even in the two poems there is a world of difference in the expression.

The matter of rhyme in poetry reading is something that is not fully understood by many readers. You should not pounce on each rhyme word as if you were a cat surprising a mouse. The rhyme word gets a little more emphasis than the other words in the line, just enough to make you conscious that there is a rhyme. Some people recite poetry in a sing-song manner, banging out the rhymed endings. No wonder they do not enjoy it. It isn't easy to read rhymed verse well, but once you can do it you will never want to go back to reading poetry silently.

A poem is frequently worth analyzing in minute detail, but, often, emotional sensitiveness is more important than analysis. In his "Poetic Principle," Poe insists on emotional sensitivity as a criterion for judging poetry. He says, "A poem deserves its title only inasmuch as it excites, by elevating the soul. The value of the poem is in the ratio of this elevating excitement." And Emily Dickinson, who has been quoted in this connection before, emphasizes the feelings of a reader of poetry when she says, "If I read a book and it makes my whole body so cold no fire can ever warm me, I know that is poetry. If I feel physically as if the top of my head were taken off, I know that is poetry. These are the only ways I know it. Is there any other way?" The meaning of the lines often sifts through the feelings they arouse. Who does not feel this as he reads through Shakespeare's sonnets? Poetry can speak to us through an endless variety of emotions. It can make us feel as if the author were so close that he is whispering in our ear.

Let poetry make its own impression on you. Do not force it to speak in any certain way. Rather, give it a chance to do its work naturally and easily. This you can do best by reading it aloud. Modern poetry, particularly, is sometimes written to appeal to the eye more than to the ear, and silent reading may be all right in such cases. Usually, however, it is the sound of the spoken voice that brings you fullest enjoyment of a poet's work.

Read poetry with an active mind, and read it aloud.

Name .... Section .... Date.............

*Record your rate here:*_____
Average rate for freshmen on Chapter 22: over 500 wpm.

application exercise: chapter 22

Reading Poetry Aloud . . .

Read the following poems softly to yourself two or three times. Then choose one and prepare to read it to your classmates.

Sonnet

The world is too much with us; late and soon,
Getting and spending, we lay waste our powers:
Little we see in nature that is ours;
We have given our hearts away, a sordid boon!
The sea that bares her bosom to the moon;
The winds that will be howling at all hours,
And are up-gathered now like sleeping flowers;
For this, for everything, we are out of tune;
It moves us not.—Great God! I'd rather be
A Pagan suckled in a creed outworn;
So might I, standing on this pleasant lea,
Have glimpses that would make me less forlorn;
Have sight of Proteus rising from the sea;
Or hear old Triton blow his wreathed horn.

William Wordsworth

Ozymandias

I met a traveler from an antique land,
Who said: Two vast and trunkless legs of stone
Stand in the desert. Near them, on the sand,
Half sunk, a shattered visage lies, whose frown,
And wrinkled lip, and sneer of cold command,
Tell that its sculptor well those passions read,
Which yet survive, stamped on these lifeless things,
The hand that mocked them, and the heart that fed:
And on the pedestal these words appear:
"My name is Ozymandias, King of Kings:
Look on my works, you Mighty, and despair!"
Nothing beside remains. Round the decay
Of that colossal wreck, boundless and bare,
The lone and level sands stretch far away.

Percy Bysshe Shelley

Constantly risking absurdity
                    and death
            whenever he performs
                    above the heads
                            of his audience
            the poet like an acrobat
                    climbs on rime
                            to a high wire of his own making
    and balancing on eyebeams
                    above a sea of faces
            paces his way
                    to the other side of day
        performing entrechats
                    and slight-of-foot tricks
    and other high theatrics
                    and all without mistaking
            any thing
                    for what it may not be
For he's the super realist
                    who must perforce perceive
            taut truth
                    before the taking of each stance of step
    in his supposed advance
                    toward the still higher perch
    where Beauty stands and waits
                            with gravity
                    to start her death-defying leap
And he
        a little charleychaplin man
                    who may or may not catch
            her fair eternal form
                    spreadeagled in the empty air
            of existence.

Lawrence Ferlinghetti

On Reading Aloud   23

Generally speaking, the chapters in this book have emphasized skillful silent reading. The title of this chapter suggests that we will here be concerned with something else. This is not true. If you can read well orally, you are very likely to read well silently, because oral reading requires much the same kind of accuracy in recognizing the meaning of words, facility in grouping the words sensibly, and sensitivity to the author's intended emphasis. Unless you transfer the slow rate of your oral reading to your silent reading, oral reading will strengthen your ability to read silently.

Very frequently, the audience is an important factor in the difference between the two types of reading. Because, when reading aloud, you are generally reading for someone, instead of for only your own inner consciousness, oral reading exacts greater accuracy from you. To avoid embarrassment before other people, you will not only take greater pains to pronounce each word correctly, which means pronouncing it as educated people in your part of the country would, but you will also try harder to make the author's meaning clear. It is not easy to fool an audience (as you may sometimes fool yourself) by rushing over a phrase or by slurring a word you cannot pronounce. You avoid doing these things, if for no other reason than to avoid criticism. The process is sometimes painful, but the fear of a scornful audience makes you toe the line, and you become a better reader because of it.

When you know someone is listening to you, you will try to read words in logical groups. Unlike primitive man (or at least the cartoonist's conception of primitive man), who probably preferred using one-word sentences, we now build complicated sentence structures of many word groups. Instead of saying, "Leave this house at once and never darken my door again," primitive man might grunt the equivalent of "Go," or he might say nothing and merely make a threatening gesture with his club. In the language you use, as you now very well know, the unit of thought is not the separate word. Rather it is the phrase or word group. When you read the sentence, "What man really wants and needs in life is an opportunity to work," you do not think of "What," then of "man," then of "really," and so forth. You think of "What-man-really-wants-and-needs-in-life," and then of the statement, "is-an-opportunity-to-work." The reading-thinking process proceeds by groups of words, not by a sequence of words following separately, one after the other.

When you are talking to someone in everyday conversation, you are establishing your thought as you go along, and to get your point across, you unconsciously group the words as clearly as you can. When you are reading aloud, however, you are not so unavoidably and directly responsible for the thoughts expressed. Because of this, you have to force your eyes to keep

93

ahead of your voice. Your eyes must move swiftly over the words on the page and organize them into groups before they are uttered. Failure to do this will mean failure to organize into clear groupings. As a result, you will fail to get the meaning across, because the meaning is derived from the groupings.

For the most part, word groups are distinguished either by punctuation or by grammatical structure. For example, the phrase "line of print" is a distinct word group that may be read almost as a single unit. In the sentence "He walked to the bookcase, picked up a book, leafed through the pages, and returned to his desk," the word groups are clearly marked by the punctuation. Occasionally, you may run into a line of print that is difficult to break into groups, because grouping changes with various conditions, but several practice readings, necessary for any passage that is difficult, should bring you through safely.

Another thing oral reading does is force you to look closely for the author's emphasis. When you write a telegram, you toss out the unnecessary frills and accessories. "Arrive Central Station 4 PM" gets the meaning across as precisely as if you said, "My train arrives at Central Station at 4 PM today." The language of the telegram may be a little more abrupt than that of the sentence, but it carries the same meaning. The illustration shows what the important words are in conveying the meaning of that particular passage, and in oral reading you stress those idea-carrying words. The rest of the words become part of the background, become words of secondary stress. If you emphasize each word of the sentence, the meaning is confused, but if you stress only those that you would use if you were putting the author's thought into a telegram, you convey the meaning clearly.

If you say, "The loveliest song I have ever heard was sung by Lily Pons," you do not stress "sung" because it is characteristic of songs to be sung. Or if you say, "The picture was painted by a man from the southern part of France," you stress *picture, man,* and *France,* and you do not emphasize the rest of the words in the sentence. You waste your energy and bore your listener by stressing the implied words. But if you subordinate them properly, you bring out the meaning as it ought to be brought out. Because clarity comes when the important things stand out from the relatively unimportant, it is just as essential for unimportant words to be suppressed as it is for the idea-carrying words to be emphasized.

The significant thing in oral reading, as in silent reading, is that you have to *think* as you read. The difference is that when you read aloud, other people are checking your thinking. The effort to deliver the author's exact meaning to them will make you a better reader.

Name .... Section .... Date ....

*Record your rate here:*_____
Average rate for freshmen on Chapter 23: over 500 wpm.

application exercise: chapter 23

Making a Speech . . .

William Faulkner, one of America's foremost authors, spoke eloquently and sincerely about the duty of a writer in his speech of acceptance upon the award of the Nobel Prize for Literature (1950). In doing so, he echoed the sentiment of Ruskin, mentioned earlier in this book, and indirectly reinforced the petition of Emerson for reading with an active mind.

Read the following speeches silently. Choose one, underline the words you think need special emphasis; prepare to deliver it to your classmates.

Nobel Prize Speech

I feel that this award was not made to me as a man, but to my work—a life's work in the agony and sweat of the human spirit, not for glory and least of all for profit, but to create out of the materials of the human spirit something which did not exist before. So this award is only mine in trust. It will not be difficult to find a dedication for the money part of it commensurate with the purpose and significance of its origin. But I would like to do the same with the acclaim too, by using this moment as a pinnacle from which I might be listened to by the young men and women already dedicated to the same anguish and travail, among whom is already that one who will some day stand here where I am standing.

Our tragedy today is a general and universal physical fear so long sustained by now that we can even bear it. There are no longer problems of the spirit. There is only the question: When will I be blown up? Because of this, the young man or woman writing today has forgotten the problems of the human heart in conflict with itself which alone can make good writing because only that is worth writing about, worth the agony and sweat.

He must learn them again. He must teach himself that the basest of all things is to be afraid; and, teaching himself that, forget it forever, leaving no room in his workshop for anything but the old verities and truths of the heart, the old universal truths lacking which any story is ephemeral and doomed—love and honor and pity and pride and compassion and sacrifice. Until he does so, he labors under a curse. He writes not of love but of lust, of defeats in which nobody loses anything of value, of victories without hope and, worst of all, without pity or compassion. His griefs grieve on no universal bones, leaving no scars. He writes not of the heart but of the glands.

Until he relearns these things, he will write as though he stood among and watched the end of man. I decline to accept the end of man. It is easy enough to say that man is immortal simply because he will endure: he will prevail. He is immortal, not because he alone among creatures has an inexhaustible voice, but because he has a soul, a spirit capable of compassion and sacrifice and endurance. The poet's, the writer's, duty is to write about these things. It is his privilege to help man endure by lifting his heart, by reminding him of the courage and honor and hope and pride and compassion and pity and sacrifice which have been the glory of his past. The poet's voice need not merely be the record of man, it can be one of the props, the pillars to help him endure and prevail. *William Faulkner*

I Am Tired of Fighting

Tell General Howard I know his heart. What he told me before I have in my heart. I am tired of fighting. Our chiefs are killed. Looking Glass is dead. Toohoolhoolzote is dead. The old men are all dead. It is the young men who say yes or no. He who led on the young men [Ollokot] is dead. It is cold and we have no blankets. The little children are freezing to death. My people, some of them, have run away to the hills, and have no blankets, no food; no one knows where they are—perhaps freezing to death. I want to have time to look for my children and see how many of them I can find. Maybe I shall find them among the dead. Hear me, my chiefs! I am tired; my heart is sick and sad. From where the sun now stands I will fight no more forever.

Chief Joseph, 1877

Why We Can't Wait

...Perhaps it is easy for those who have never felt the stinging darts of segregation to say, "Wait." But when you have seen vicious mobs lynch your mothers and fathers at will and drown your sisters and brothers at whim; when you have seen hate-filled policemen curse, kick, and even kill your black brothers and sisters; when you see the vast majority of your twenty million Negro brothers smothering in an airtight cage of poverty in the midst of an affluent society; when you suddenly find your tongue twisted and your speech stammering as you seek to explain to your six-year-old daughter why she can't go to the public amusement park that has just been advertised on television, and see tears welling up in her eyes when she is told that Funtown is closed to colored children, and see ominous clouds of inferiority beginning to form in her little mental sky, and see her beginning to distort her personality by developing an unconscious bitterness toward white people; when you have to concoct an answer for a five-year-old son who is asking: "Daddy, why do white people treat colored people so mean?"; when you take a cross-country drive and find it necessary to sleep night after night in the uncomfortable corners of your automobile because no motel will accept you; when you are humiliated day in and day out by nagging signs reading "white" and "colored"; when your first name becomes "nigger," your middle name becomes "boy" (however old you are) and your last name becomes "John," and your wife and mother are never given the respected title "Mrs."; when you are harried by day and haunted by night by the fact that you are a Negro, living constantly at tiptoe stance, never quite knowing what to expect next, and are plagued with inner fears and outer resentments; when you are forever fighting a degenerating sense of "nobodiness"—then you will understand why we find it difficult to wait. There comes a time when the cup of endurance runs over, and men are no longer willing to be plunged into the abyss of despair. *Martin Luther King, Jr.*

Choosing Your Reading 24

Throughout this book you have been learning to become a skillful reader. You have found out how to overcome your bad reading habits by forcing good ones to take their place. You have some knowledge about various reading skills, from skimming to training in comprehension—knowledge that is important because it helps you to become an efficient reader. But the teaching of efficient reading is not the only purpose of this book. By learning how to read *better* you should have a strong desire to read *more*—more *good* books.

There are so many good books that it is impossible to read them all—even if we devoted twenty-four hours a day to the task. So we are forced to be selective. Knowing it is impossible to read all we should like to, our concern is to choose the best.

Useful publications to turn to in a search for the best contemporary books are the major magazines and the Sunday book review sections of such large metropolitan newspapers as the *New York Times*. The Sunday book review section of the *New York Times* is perhaps the most generally available. In these publications appear critical comments by qualified reviewers on books published during the week. The business of the reviewers is to read a new book, digest it, and tell the world whether or not it is worth reading.

Reviews in current newspapers and magazines are valuable for criticism of the latest books. Suppose, however, you pick up a book on a topic that interests you, *Penetrating the Mind*, published a number of years ago, and you wish to find out what the critical opinion of the book is. A useful publication, the *Book Review Digest,* will serve your purpose. Of course, you could read back copies of a single magazine that reviews books weekly or monthly, but the *Book Review Digest,* which provides a selection of critical opinion from all the important sources of reviews, is a much more convenient instrument to use. Each year a large selection of book reviews on every subject is included in this publication. You need only to find the volume for the year in which *Penetrating the Mind* was published to learn what the favorable and unfavorable opinions were. The *Book Review Digest* attempts to present a cross-section of opinion, usually limited to brief comments that indicate each critic's capsule opinion of the book.

For contemporary books, then, see the criticisms in the magazines, the Sunday *New York Times*, or the *Book Review Digest*. For the best books among the classics, turn to those recommended in the pocketbook, *Good Reading* which was published under the auspices of the National Council of Teachers of English. Many of these recommended books will provide you with stimulating reading. To be sure, there are very few adventure stories or "whodunits" on their list, but the *Good Reading* guide, as well as books chosen by the Great Books Foundation, includes books that will set you to thinking more deeply than you usually do when you read. A sure mark of an educated man is his familiarity with the ideas in the great books.

Remember that the popularity of a book does not make it great. And unless it concerns some controversial matter its popularity may not even make it a worthy topic of conversation. It is foolish, therefore, to read the most popular books on the best-seller list just to have something to talk about. It happens, unfortunately, that a number of them don't amount to very much in the long run. If you were to review the best sellers for the past fifty years, you would find that many of the most popular have been forgotten. For example, the novels of authors like E. P. Roe and Mrs. E.D.E.N. Southworth, which were best sellers at the turn of the century, are very seldom mentioned in any of the surveys of our literary culture. There are books for the hour and books for the ages. If you value your time, choose wisely when you select your literary company.

The great books of our own age, those that have exerted a profound influence on our time, are very few. Even if you have not read them, you should be aware of the force and power of such books as the *Bible* and the works of Charles Darwin, Karl Marx, and Sigmund Freud. In these books you will find ideas that form the nucleus of the molding forces of our age.

Each member of the advisory board of *Good Reading* submitted a personal list of basic books that he would buy first if his library were somehow destroyed. Many of the old favorites, such as Shakespeare, the *Bible,* Homer, Plato, Montaigne, Tolstoy, and Melville, were mentioned, but it is interesting to note that H.G. Well's *Outline of History* was listed as frequently as many of the others in this sampling of the literary sympathies of modern American writers. The lists were drawn up by men like John Dos Passos, Clifton Fadiman, John Hersey, and Carl Sandburg; and if these books proved "basic" to them, they ought to prove good reading for us.

Choose your books as you would choose your friends: have a speaking acquaintance with many; be on intimate terms with a few; be on the lookout for new ones and hold fast to the old ones you have found worthy. Some books, like some people, are not worth knowing well. Usually it is not necessary to be with a bad man long to know what he is like. Neither is it necessary to read a poor book all the way through. Some books, like some friends, are worth visiting frequently; we never cease to enjoy their company.

Choose your books wisely and read them well. Enter the world of books with an open and inquiring mind, and it will share with you a wealth that is beyond measuring.

Good reading to you!

Name .... Section .... Date............

*Record your rate here:*_____
Average rate for freshmen on Chapter 24: over 500 wpm.

application exercise: chapter 24

Recalling What's Happened . . .

Allow ten minutes for this test covering important points in Reading Skills. In front of each item write T for true or F for false. Each of the ten true items counts ten points, and a perfect score is 100. The answer key is on page 100.

1. In college about 15 per cent of all study activity involves the reading process.
2. If you are reading over 200 words per minute, the chances are you are a word-by-word reader.
3. You need not worry about straining your eyes by reading at very rapid rates unless you wear glasses.
4. A good reading distance for most people is 14 to 16 inches from the eyes.
5. Most good books these days are printed on bright, white paper and in clear, black type.
6. A reader makes a regression when he tries to translate a single word into a meaningful idea.
7. The number of fixations depends on the difficulty of the material and not the purpose of the reader.
8. The amount of time spent in moving the eyes is about the same amount needed to make fixations.
9. One of the main factors in the difference between oral and silent reading is the audience.
10. You should use a constant rate when reading a textbook in order to understand each section equally well.
11. The signposts of a book refer only to chapter headings and subheadings.
12. Doctors have determined with scientific accuracy how habits are formed.
13. Learning words in context is the best and easiest way to improve your vocabulary.
14. Because reading is an important study aid, all reading habits should be kept, even at the cost of breaking others.
15. The two main kinds of vocabulary are: (1) vocabulary of a textbook and (2) vocabulary of a newspaper.
16. The dictionary usually establishes one standard meaning for a word.
17. The average reading rate for adults is 250 to 300 words per minute.
18. People have been known to read 4000 words per minute.
19. If you set up a reading program for yourself, plan to spend at least 2 to 4 hours a day on it.
20. It is sufficient to practice increasing your rate of reading by spending one full period a week on it. *should be daily.*
21. A successful reading rate improvement program can be accomplished in a month or two.
22. In an outline the main ideas are usually set off by Arabic numerals.
23. It is not a good idea, in fact it is illogical, to look at the conclusion of the section or chapter before beginning to read it.

F 24. Skimming by an automatic or mechanical process (e.g., reading every fourth page) is particularly efficient.

T 25. If you have a question in mind and, using the index and chapter headings, read to find the answer, you will be skimming well.

F 26. When you skim you read everything faster than usual.

27. It is inefficient to skim a whole magazine before reading it thoroughly.

28. It is important to read groups of words; never, even on a crucial passage, examine each word as you read.

T 29. The supreme test of a skillful reader is his ability to read critically and creatively.

F 30. A poor reader often makes four to five fixations per line.

F 31. Forcing yourself to read more carefully will make it possible to turn hearing into seeing.

F 32. In a reading program to increase rate, you read just beyond your comfortable rate.

F 33. Too often a book becomes messy and less useful if you write in it.

34. It is usually best when taking notes to jot down direct quotations.

35. A good summary includes all the facts and examples that prove the author's point.

36. The only real standard of an author's language should be the degree of its clarity.

37. If you write only the concluding sentences of an article, you will have a fair summary of its contents.

38. Poetry should be read silently and with deep thought, not emotionally.

39. The rhyme word in a line of poetry should get a very decided emphasis when you read it aloud.

40. When you read a work of great literature for the first time, you should relax and read for sheer enjoyment.

41. It is better to have chosen the wrong theme or unifying principle of a book as you are reading it than to choose none at all.

42. The opinions of astute professional critics determine whether a book is good or bad or something between good and bad.

43. When you dissect a book part by part, you destroy some of the beauty of the whole and the impact of its unity.

44. It is possible and often desirable when analyzing to state the theme of a very long book in a dozen words or so.

45. A reader who constantly challenges the author's purpose in putting one part of a book before another gains understanding but loses aesthetic enjoyment.

46. The public library, because it is widely used, has a tremendous impact on American life.

47. The Reader's Guide to Periodical Literature issues a bi-annual index of most of the magazines in America.

48. The first step in looking up a topic in the library would normally be to go to the call desk.

49. Those who read well orally usually cannot read as well silently.

50. Transferring the rate of your oral reading to silent reading will strengthen your ability to read silently.

True statements are 4, 9, 13, 17, 25, 29, 32, 40, 41, 44.

Comprehension Checks

comprehension check: chapter 1

Write the letters of the best answers in the blanks. Key appears with Comprehension Check 3.

1. In college, the percentage of all study activity involving the reading process is:
   (a) 50%   (c) 75%
   (b) 85%   (d) 65%   *b*   c

2. To learn to comprehend better you should learn to read:
   (a) each word separately   (c) in whole phrases
   (b) each word symbolically   (d) none of these   *c*   a

3. If you read much it is important to:
   (a) have your glasses checked regularly
   (b) wear your glasses only when reading
   (c) wear reading glasses
   (d) glasses not mentioned   *d*   d

4. It is true that when you read fast:
   (a) you cannot comprehend as accurately
   (b) you cannot retain as long
   (c) you can understand as much as when you read slowly
   (d) none of these   *c*   c

5. Skillful reading requires:
   (a) good illumination   (c) efficient eye movements
   (b) good reading environment   (d) none of these mentioned   *d*

6. Formal teaching of reading usually ceases after:
   (a) elementary grades   (c) senior high grades
   (b) junior high grades   (d) subject not mentioned   *a*   c

7. You may infer from this chapter that an important aspect of reading is the reader's:
   (a) past experience   (c) perception of the author   *a*/
   (b) span of reading   (d) sensitivity   *c*

8. Performance in rational learning: a
   (a) increases with maturity   (c) has no effect on reading   *a*/
   (b) decreases with maturity   (d) subject not mentioned   *d*

9. When you read you should:
   (a) keep in mind the main idea   c
   (b) relate important items to the main idea
   (c) draw a conclusion and relate your reading to your background
   (d) do all of these things   *d*

10. The efficient reader reads faster than: b
    (a) 500 wpm (words per minute)   (c) 2000 wpm
    (b) 100 wpm   (d) subject not mentioned   *d*   d

d

comprehension check: chapter 2

Write the letters of the best answers in the blanks. Key appears with Comprehension Check 24.

1. Your reading habits are conditioned by:
   (a) physical attributes   (c) personality factors
   (b) mental skills   (d) all of these   *d*

c
2. A word-by-word reader probably reads slower than:
   (a) 100 wpm   (c) 200 wpm
   (b) 150 wpm   (d) subject not mentioned   *c*

a
3. Eliminate lip reading by:
   (a) thrusting a pencil between your teeth
   (b) sticking a knuckle in your mouth
   (c) neither of these
   (d) either of these   *a* ✓

a
4. The reading skill that can be developed very quickly is:
   (a) vocabulary   (c) speed
   (b) comprehension   (d) eye movements   *d* ✓

c
5. Vocabulary can be improved by:
   (a) alertness and ability to concentrate
   (b) drill, discipline, and practice
   (c) testing frequently
   (d) subject not mentioned   *d* ✓

d
6. You can become conscious of pronouncing each word in your throat by:
   (a) looking at yourself in a mirror
   (b) having a friend watch you read
   (c) feeling your throat with your fingers
   (d) none of these   *c*

c
7. For the most part comprehension depends on:
   (a) drill, discipline, and practice on magazine articles
   (b) alertness and the ability to concentrate
   (c) reading at a good speed; avoiding word-by-word reading

c
   (d) none of these   *b*

8. You cannot read well if you:
   (a) read in bed
   (b) listen to the radio at the same time

a
   (c) read in a moving vehicle
   (d) none of these mentioned   *d*

9. This chapter deals mainly with:
   (a) obstacles in the path of efficient reading

c
   (b) how to survey your reading habits
   (c) how to increase your speed of reading
   (d) none of these   *b*

d
10. You may infer from this chapter that a survey of your present reading habits is:
   (a) far more   (c) far less
   (b) slightly more   (d) slightly less   *a*
   important in a reading efficiency program than making a determined effort to increase the amount of reading you do.

comprehension check: chapter 3

Write the letters of the best answers in the blanks. Key appears with Comprehension Check 5.

1. This chapter is mainly about:
   (*a*) reading hazards
   (*b*) keeping in good shape for skillful reading
   (*c*) how to take care of your eyes while reading   *b*
   (*d*) none of these

   b

2. The best kind of paper for printed matter is:
   (*a*) dull white   (*c*) pure white
   (*b*) shiny white   (*d*) none of these   *a*

   c

3. In general, the health of your eyes ordinarily depends on:
   (*a*) your diet
   (*b*) eye exercises
   (*c*) the over-all health of your body   d
   (*d*) proper care of your visual organs   *c*

4. You should have your eyes checked:
   (*a*) before you begin school
   (*b*) when you enter an occupation that requires close reading
   (*c*) at regular intervals   c
   (*d*) both *b* and *c*   *C*

5. Some people have become dizzy when reading:
   (*a*) aboard ships   (*c*) in taxicabs   d
   (*b*) in an airplane   (*d*) none of these mentioned   *d*

6. The best position for a book you are reading is:
   (*a*) flat on the table or desk   (*c*) in an inclined position   a
   (*b*) upright in your hand   (*d*) not mentioned   *c*

7. When reading, avoid a strained or twitching feeling about the eyes by:
   (*a*) looking at some distant object from time to time
   (*b*) massaging the eyes carefully   a
   (*c*) getting glasses to correct defects of vision
   (*d*) none of these mentioned   *a*

8. Most people hold a book so that the distance from the eyes is: a
   (*a*) 11 to 13 inches   (*c*) 17 to 19 inches
   (*b*) 14 to 16 inches   (*d*) none of these mentioned   *b*

9. Students who read eight or more hours a day have no eye fatigue because they:
   (*a*) concentrate intensively   (*c*) read rapidly, in whole phrases
   (*b*) are used to reading   (*d*) none of these mentioned   *d*   d

10. When you try to read yourself to sleep you:
    (*a*) ruin your eyes
    (*b*) relax too much   d
    (*c*) break training rules for efficient reading
    (*d*) none of these mentioned   *d*   ✓

comprehension check: chapter 4

Write the letters of the best answers in the blanks. Key appears with Comprehension Check 2.

1. The eyes move across a line of print:
   (a) in one smooth even movement   (c) in starts and stops
c   (b) by going backward and forward   (d) none of these   _____

2. The number of fixations a slow reader makes per line is:
   (a) 10 to 12   (c) 3 to 5
a   (b) 15 to 17   (d) none of these   _____

3. The amount of time spent moving the eyes as compared to the amount of time to make a fixation is:
c   (a) shorter   (c) longer
    (b) the same   (d) subject not mentioned   _____

4. One of the best ways to improve eye movements is to practice:
b   (a) on an eye-exercise sheet
    (b) on an instrument
    (c) reading light, interesting material
b   (d) none of these   _____

5. Regressions are caused by:
   (a) eye strain   (c) twitching eyes
d   (b) poor illumination   (d) none of these mentioned   _____

6. In comparison to the first page, the class of freshmen who read the second page in half the time:
d   (a) concentrated almost as intensively
    (b) improved their eye movements
    (c) remembered almost as much
a   (d) concentrated much more intensively   _____

7. The number of fixations depends upon:
   (a) the difficulty of the material   (c) both of these
c   (b) the purpose of the reader   (d) neither of these   _____

8. When a reader, like a typist, begins to consider individual words, he:
   (a) becomes less efficient   (c) makes fewer errors
   (b) becomes more painstaking   (d) subject not mentioned   _____

c 9. When you read familiar material over and over again against time, you:
   (a) become bored with it
   (b) see new meanings
   (c) see new, logical groupings of words
   (d) subject not mentioned   _____

10. You will be able to read more efficiently if you:
    (a) are conscious of eye movements   (c) apply both of these
    (b) exercise your eyes diligently   (d) neither of these   _____

comprehension check: chapter 5

Write the letters of the best answers in the blanks. Key appears with Comprehension Check 7.

1. The main idea of this chapter is:
   (a) concentrate intensively   (c) read rapidly
   (b) comprehend accurately   (d) none of these   _____

2. You read slowly a technical work on a subject with which you are not very
   familiar because you need to:
   (a) absorb the style   (c) learn new vocabulary
   (b) take notes   (d) both b and c   _____

3. When you read for enrichment of life, you read:
   (a) with undivided attention   (c) both of these
   (b) slowly and with caution   (d) subject not mentioned _____

4. When you read for the author's general trend of thought, you read:
   (a) rapidly   (c) both of these
   (b) slowly and carefully   (d) subject not mentioned _____

5. If you tried to read a number of biographies of any one person, you would:
   (a) read them all slowly
   (b) read the last ones more rapidly
   (c) read them all rapidly
   (d) subject not mentioned   _____

6. To locate information on a historical figure in a large history book, you would:
   (a) read the whole book swiftly (c) read the whole book slowly
   (b) use the glossary   (d) none of these   _____

7. Rapid reading helps decrease:
   (a) eye strain   (c) both of these
   (b) twitching eyes   (d) subject not mentioned _____

8. The term *shifting gears,* as used in this chapter, refers to changing:
   (a) degree of concentration   (c) speed of reading
   (b) the purpose of your reading (d) none of these   _____

9. You may assume from reading this chapter that:
   (a) there is no correct speed of reading
   (b) reading is strictly individual
   (c) both of these
   (d) neither of these   _____

10. A popularized version of your topic allows you to:
    (a) shift into low   (c) coast along
    (b) shift into second   (d) subject not mentioned _____

b

a

c

c

d

c

a

b

d

c

comprehension check: chapter 6

Write the letters of the best answers in the blanks. Key appears with Comprehension Check 4.

1. The chief rule for skimming is:
   (a) move rapidly   (c) read for a purpose
   (b) comprehend accurately   (d) none of these   _____

a
2. To find specific information listed in the *World Almanac,* turn first to the:
   (a) index   (c) glossary
   (b) table of contents   (d) none of these   _____

3. The sports page of a newspaper usually:
   (a) follows the business section   (c) is in the same location
   (b) follows the comics   (d) subject not mentioned   _____

a
4. The publication that lends itself most readily to skimming is the:
   (a) pamphlet   (c) popular novel
   (b) newspaper   (d) subject not mentioned   _____

c
5. You can get a good clue to a magazine story's plot by:
   (a) looking at the pictures   (c) neither of these
   (b) reading the subtitles   (d) subject not mentioned   _____

a
6. Skimming a book is like:
   (a) skimming a flat rock over water   (c) both of these
   (b) skimming cream off milk   (d) neither of these   _____

c
7. The publication which prints all the news that's fit to print is:
   (a) the *New York Times*   (c) The *Christian Science Monitor*
   (b) the *Chicago Tribune*   (d) publication not mentioned   _____

c
8. You skim when you are reading:
   (a) the headlines   (c) the picture page
   (b) the comics   (d) none of these   _____

9. Important items to efficient skimmers are:
   (a) chapter headings   (c) both of these
   (b) subheadings   (d) neither of these   _____

c
10. You can infer from reading this chapter that in normal reading (that is, not skimming) you:
   (a) read word for word   (c) do not omit portions
   (b) group words   (d) none of these   _____

b

d

d

comprehension check: chapter 7

Write the letters of the best answers in the blanks. Key appears with Comprehension Check 9.

1. This chapter is mainly about:
   (a) good comprehension   (c) both of these
   (b) rapid reading   (d) neither of these   _c_ d

2. A good illustration of reading intensively is offered by readers of:
   (a) comic books   (c) long novels
   (b) scholarly essays   (d) none of these   _____ c

3. Cure yourself of daydreaming when you read by:
   (a) forcing yourself to read intensively
   (b) skipping a few pages
   (c) sleeping a little while   c
   (d) none of these   _____

4. One way to learn to concentrate is by:
   (a) reading the same material over and over   a
   (b) reading late at night
   (c) reading in the same place
   (d) none of these   _____

5. You may have difficulty concentrating if:
   (a) the lighting is bad   (c) both of these are true b
   (b) your glasses need adjusting (d) neither of these mentioned _____

6. To improve concentration:
   (a) read for a definite purpose (c) read to get out of a rut d
   (b) read to broaden your knowledge (d) none of these   _____

7. Two men who tried to concentrate in cork-lined chambers were:
   (a) Carlyle and Poe   (c) Carlyle and Proust   d
   (b) Poe and Chaucer   (d) Chaucer and Proust   _____

8. The principle factor in good concentration is:
   (a) good lighting and comfort (c) a quiet place to work   c
   (b) self-discipline and conditioning (d) none of these   _____

9. This chapter recommends that you learn to concentrate at:
   (a) a table in the public library (c) neither of these places
   (b) your desk in your study   (d) either of these places _____

10. This chapter suggests you read: c
    (a) rapidly   (c) both of these
    (b) for comprehension   (d) neither of these mentioned _____

                                                              c

comprehension check: chapter 8

Write the letters of the best answers in the blanks. Key appears with Comprehension Check 6.

1. This chapter emphasizes:
   (a) discarding the unneeded and retaining the valuable
   (b) using the index or table of contents
   (c) using the preface or introduction
   d (d) rereading and discussing a book   *a*

2. Perhaps the difficulty of a poor reader is that he:
   (a) fails to relate generalizations and details
   a (b) reads hesitatingly
   (c) reads too rapidly
   (d) none of these   *a*

3. The point made about the autistic child is that:
   (a) a therapy was found   (c) therapy is not a full answer
   b (b) a therapy was not found   (d) there is no therapy   *a*

4. The statement, "Youth, as a rule, has an immense reserve of strength," is a:
   (a) generalization   (c) supporting statement
   c (b) rule   (d) subject not mentioned   *a*

5. A paragraph topic sentence:
   (a) concludes a unit of development   (c) is both of these
   a (b) begins a unit of development   (d) is always the first sentence   *c*

6. When a reader, looking for particular information, has found the part of the book in which it is located, he can:
   a (a) skim for key words   (c) both of these
   (b) subordinate less relevant facts   (d) neither of these   *a*

7. The sign of a successful executive is:
   d (a) an empty wastebasket at the start of the day
   (b) a full wastebasket at the end of the day
   (c) both of these
   c (d) neither of these   *c*

8. To comprehend well you must be able to:
   (a) skim rapidly and concentrate   (c) use your eyes intelligently
   (b) use the sign-post technique   (d) none of these   *a*

9. Rapid reading of light, interesting material helps:
   a (a) improve eye movements   (c) both of these
   (b) concentration   (d) subject not mentioned   _____

10. You can infer that good comprehension depends upon:
    (a) mental alertness
    (b) ability to sift the chaff from the wheat
    d (c) ability to use the sign-post technique
    (d) all of these   _____

comprehension check: chapter 9

Write the letters of the best answers in the blanks. Key appears with Comprehension Check 11.

1. This chapter urges as a cure for forgetfulness:
   (a) reading a textbook on psychology
   (b) taking a memory-training course
   (c) looking for the thread of unity   d
   (d) all of these   _____

2. It is often helpful to find the relationship of the parts by:
   (a) doing what the true murder-mystery does   (c) neither of these   a
   (b) looking at the end of a section or chapter   (d) both of these   _____

3. You can remember more easily if you:
   (a) choose good reading environment
   (b) read good books rapidly
   (c) both of these   a
   (d) neither of these mentioned   _____

4. Puritans could remember the details of Calvin's doctrines because:
   (a) the conclusion was a driving force in everyone's life
   (b) the conclusion was built upon a chronological succession of events
   (c) both of these   c
   (d) neither of these   _____

5. In regard to the unifying principle, this chapter says it is better to:
   (a) choose the wrong one than none at all   d
   (b) choose one based on chronology
   (c) choose one based on trends
   (d) none of these   _____   a

6. Your memory is influenced by:
   (a) nerve centers   (c) neither of these
   (b) special stimuli   (d) both of these   _____   c

7. If your memory is pushed far enough by the act of rejection or denial you will be forced to:
   (a) challenge the author's integrity   (c) find the true conception   b
   (b) put the book aside for a while   (d) none of these   _____

8. A created being:
   (a) cannot impose its will on whoever created it   d
   (b) exists by a unifying principle
   (c) both of these
   (d) subject not mentioned   _____   d

9. Forgetfulness is caused by:
   (a) carelessness   (c) both of these
   (b) poor concentration   (d) neither of these   _____

10. This chapter says that some men can:
    (a) memorize Shakespeare
    (b) memorize a page of a dictionary
    (c) memorize whole pages of a telephone book
    (d) none of these   _____

comprehension check: chapter 10

Write the letters of the best answers in the blanks. Key appears with Comprehension Check 8.

1. Habits are:
   (*a*) begun by a stimulus
d (*b*) formed by impulses traveling to a nerve center
   (*c*) well-trod paths formed by impulses
   (*d*) all of these   _____

2. Nerve impulses begin by:
   (*a*) unknown causes   (*c*) fluctuating rapidly
d (*b*) inherited characteristics   (*d*) subject not mentioned   _____

3. You keep habits:
   (*a*) because you can't get rid of them
a (*b*) unless you have reason to change
   (*c*) neither of these
   (*d*) subject not mentioned   _____

4. Habits:
   (*a*) make movements exact   (*c*) both of these
b (*b*) lessen fatigue   (*d*) neither of these mentioned   _____

5. A child learning to tie his shoes illustrates:
   (*a*) trial-and-error method   (*c*) neither of these
   (*b*) a creature of habit   (*d*) subject not mentioned   _____

6. Habits that reduce the attention with which acts are performed:
a (*a*) are useful   (*c*) should be eliminated
   (*b*) are symptoms of carelessness   (*d*) both *b* and *c*   _____

7. Mr. *X* increased his number of words per minute from:
c (*a*) 400 to 800   (*c*) 250 to 850
   (*b*) 300 to 700   (*d*) 300 to 800   _____

8. Mr. *X* showed a big increase after the tenth or twelfth day because:
   (*a*) he had broken old habits (*c*) both of these
   (*b*) he had formed new habits (*d*) subject not mentioned   _____

b 9. If Mr. *X* stopped practicing after the tenth period, he would:
   (*a*) soon revert to old habits
   (*b*) stay at that level
   (*c*) go beyond that level
   (*d*) none of these mentioned   _____

d 10. Mr. *X* succeeded because:
   (*a*) he had a strong desire to succeed
   (*b*) he practiced regularly
d (*c*) he made his habits automatic
   (*d*) all of these   _____

c

comprehension check: chapter 11

Match the following. Not all the items in the left-hand column can be matched; none is used twice. Key appears with Comprehension Check 13.

(a) thick, heavy lines
(b) this, that
(c) Dickens and Kipling
(d) stream-of-consciousness
(e) Dos Passos and Faulkner
(f) first and last paragraphs
(g) used for afterthoughts
(h) Roman numerals
(i) for reference to one topic
(j) indicate contrast
(k) punctuation, type, and special words
(l) colon and semicolon
(m) Arabic numerals
(n) table of contents
(o) instrumentation

1. tricks of typography used by _____ c
2. italics sometimes used to show _____
3. boldface _____ _a_ b
4. reference words _____ _i_
5. dash _____
6. indicate main ideas in an outline _____ _n_
7. give idea of purpose _____ _f_ d
8. use index _____
9. however, yet _____
10. mechanical aids _____ _k_

a

a

d

d

a

d

c

comprehension check: chapter 12

Write the letters of the best answers in the blanks. Key appears with Comprehension Check 10.

d

1. A dictionary will usually offer:
   (a) clues to context   (c) clues to rapier words
   (b) one precise meaning for a word   (d) a choice of meanings   _____

c

2. This chapter advises you to:
   (a) buy a dictionary
   (b) use a dictionary daily
   (c) learn new words from a dictionary
   (d) browse in a dictionary   _____

3. The best method of enriching your vocabulary is to:
   (a) learn words while reading   (c) learn word lists
   (b) talk to many people   (d) none of these   _____

a

4. Context means:
   (a) roots and prefixes of surrounding words
   (b) surrounding words which add to meaning
   (c) words that sound like one thing but mean something else
   (d) words used like synonyms   _____

a

5. The voters were confused about celibacy because they:
   (a) heard "accused" and "deliberately"
   (b) thought it meant "an unmarried state"
   (c) both of these
   (d) thought the senator a scoundrel   _____

c

6. The man who spoke about the test of a democracy was:
   (a) Norman Thomas   (c) Norman Cousins
   (b) Thomas Mann   (d) Sinclair Lewis   _____

a

7. Everyone knows the final words of Patrick Henry's speech. The first ones are:
   (a) "Why stand we here idle?"
   (b) "Gentlemen may cry peace"
   (c) "Is life so dear or peace so sweet?"
   (d) "The war is actually begun"   _____

c

8. An important basis for judging a person ought to be:
   (a) the size of his vocabulary
   (b) the equality of his vocabulary
   (c) his level of attainment
   (d) how actively he tries to better himself   _____

b

9. Words used as tools of criticism are:
   (a) rapier words   (c) both of these
   (b) broadsword words   (d) neither of these   _____

c

10. You will probably know how to use a word later if you learn it:
    (a) in a word list   (c) in context
    (b) in school of college (d) none of these   _____

d

114

comprehension check: chapter 13

Write the letters of the best answers in the blanks. Key appears with Comprehension Check 15.

1. The best notes are taken when you use:
   (a) pencil   (c) typewriter
   (b) ink   (d) none of these mentioned _____d_____

2. This chapter suggests you take notes by:
   (a) using index cards   (c) writing in the book
   (b) using a notebook   (d) any and all of these _____d_____

3. The man who usually makes an index for his books is
   (a) John Erskine   (c) Norman Cousins
   (b) Erskine Caldwell   (d) Robert Hutchins _____a_____

4. When you take notes in a book, it is a good idea to:
   (a) underline key statements   (c) write in the margin
   (b) use colored pencils   (d) all of these _____h_____

5. A good general rule for note-taking is to:
   (a) quote the author always
   (b) put it in your own words always
   (c) quote the author if he puts it in a memorable way
   (d) write it in a memorable way yourself _____d_____

6. When you take notes, record:
   (a) page number, author, and title   (o) the time you took the notes
   (b) your location when you took notes (d) all of these _____a_____

7. The form of your notes may be:
   (a) as an outline or summary   (c) on different colored papers
   (b) on different size cards   (d) all of these _____a_____

8. When you take notes, concentrate on:
   (a) the author's organization   (c) both of these
   (b) the author's phrasing   (d) neither of these _____c_____

9. Notes help you:
   (a) retain information
   (b) keep a permanent record
   (c) when giving a long and detailed speech before an audience
   (d) both a and b _____h_____

10. When you take notes in the margin of a book, write a:
    (a) clear phrasing of a major topic
    (b) comment of your own
    (c) question the author failed to answer
    (d) any or all of these _____

e
d
a
b
g
h
f
i
j
k

comprehension check: chapter 14

Write the letters of the best answers in the blanks. Key appears with Comprehension Check 12.

1. When you summarize, you must:
   (a) understand the main ideas and their relationship
   (b) record key points in connected form
   (c) choose an economical and exact method of expression
   (d) all of these   *b* ✓

d

2. You will have a fair summary of an article if you write:
   (a) the first two paragraphs
   (b) the last two paragraphs
   (c) the topic sentence of each paragraph
   (d) the topic sentence of every third paragraph   *c*

c

3. When you write a summary for your own use, you:
   (a) abbreviate long words and leave out some short ones
   (b) omit dates and titles you already know
   (c) add implications of your own
   (d) all of these   *d* ✓

d

4. To make good summaries, you must make decisions about:
   (a) the author's plan and key ideas
   (b) your purpose in the light of the author's purpose
   (c) the author's style of writing
   (d) all of these   *a*

d

5. An effective method of testing the worth of your summary is to:
   (a) try it out on a sympathetic friend
   (b) try it out on another book by the same author
   (c) set it aside for a month or two
   (d) none of these   *c*

a

6. You may infer that a summary should:
   (a) include all essential information   (d) both a and b
   (b) serve your purpose equally as well as the author's
   (c) include the entire last paragraph   *d* ✓

d

7. Many a young writer has been advised to:
   (a) live near the writer's best market, New York City
   (b) become more mature before attempting an ambitious work
   (c) let his material age
   (d) subject not mentioned   *d* ✓

b

8. Your final summary should reflect clearly:
   (a) your opinion of the subject   (c) the wheat and the chaff
   (b) what the author said   (d) both b and c   *b*

c

9. A good example of a summary, according to this chapter, is a:
   (a) battle report of a general   (d) none of these
   (b) policeman's report of an accident
   (c) student's summary of a term paper   *c*

10. An author usually includes a summary of his book:
    (a) on the dust jacket or cover   (c) in the introduction
    (b) in the preface   (d) none of these mentioned   *d*

b

comprehension check: chapter 15

Match the following. Not all the items in the left-hand column can be matched; none is used twice. Key appears with Comprehension Check 17.

(a) subject, author, location

(b) *The Saturday Review* and *The Nation*

(c) date of publication

(d) table of contents

(e) call desk

(f) Englishmen

(g) card catalog

(h) author, title, call number

(i) Union Catalog

(j) *The Atlantic* and *The Saturday Review*

(k) *Poole's Index to Periodical Literature*

(l) 10

(m) 20

(n) 48

(o) 70

(p) 90

(q) 100

(r) subject, title, author

(s) *Harper's* and *The Atlantic*

(t) librarians

(u) publishers' list

(v) Kardex Visible File

(w) subject card

(x) *Newsweek* and *Redbook*

(y) *The Reader's Guide* to *Periodical Literature*

1. What percentage of libraries were built by Carnegie? _____

2. What percentage of people did not read a book in a 3-year period? _____

3. What lists each book in the library? _____

4. Under what headings are books listed in the library? _____

5. Where should investigation of magazines begin? _____

6. What magazines are mentioned for a good analysis of a subject? _____

7. What magazines are mentioned for a good popular treatment of a subject? _____

8. Where do you look if you can't remember the author or title of a book? _____

9. How many millions are strangers to the library? _____

10. Who are critical of Americans? _____

comprehension check: chapter 16

Write the letters of the best answers in the blanks. Key appears with Comprehension Check 14.

1. This chapter states that doctors, because of their long training, are:
   - (a) careful and analytical readers
   - (c) both of these
   - (b) fast and skillful readers
   - (d) neither of these _c (d)_

c

2. Find more time to read by organizing yourself and:
   - (a) providing yourself with sufficient reading material
   - (b) cutting out movies, television, and unnecessary activities
   - (c) improving your reading habits
   - (d) none of these _c_

b

3. Successful people, according to this chapter:
   - (a) have little time for reading
   - (b) travel widely and meet many people
   - (c) have achieved financial goals
   - (d) budget their time _d_

a

4. This chapter advises you not to:
   - (a) read comics
   - (c) listen to daytime serials
   - (b) watch television
   - (d) none of these _d_

a

5. The average rate of reading for adults is:
   - (a) 100 to 150 wpm
   - (c) 200 to 250 wpm
   - (b) 150 to 200 wpm
   - (d) 250 to 300 wpm _d_

d

6. A high school boy read *Northwest Passage* at:
   - (a) 1200 wpm
   - (c) 800 wpm
   - (b) 1000 wpm
   - (d) 600 wpm _a_

7. People have been known to read:
   - (a) 1200 wpm
   - (c) 1800 wpm
   - (b) 1500 wpm
   - (d) over 2000 wpm _d_

c

8. A number of people have increased their efficiency and doubled their reading rate in:
   - (a) two weeks
   - (c) six weeks
   - (b) four weeks
   - (d) eight weeks _b_

c

9. For most people, energy is at a low ebb:
   - (a) an hour or so after arising
   - (b) just before lunch
   - (c) an hour or two before the evening meal
   - (d) none of these _d_ ✓

b
c

f 10. You can infer from this chapter that a vacation from a reading program after the first week or two:
   - (a) rests your eyes
   - (b) allows a regression to old habits
   - (c) conserves your energy
   - (d) none of these _b_

118

comprehension check: chapter 17

Write the letters of the best answers in the blanks. Key appears with Comprehension Check 19.

1. Lowell said:
   - (a) "Some books should be digested"   m
   - (b) "Books are the treasured wealth of the world"
   - (c) "Few men learn the highest use of books"
   - (d) "A good book is the precious life-blood of a master-spirit"   _____ n

2. The man who attributes to curiosity most of the important scientific contribution is:
   - (a) Sir Isaac Newton   (c) Abraham Flexner   g
   - (b) Galileo   (d) Albert Einstein   *a*   r

3. This chapter tries to tell the reader, mainly:
   - (a) how to read   (c) where and what to read   y
   - (b) why to read   (d) all of these   *h*
   s

4. This chapter suggests you read to:
   - (a) experience and converse
   - (b) face the future and forget past history
   - (c) develop curiosity and factual knowledge   x
   - (d) none of these   *c*

Match the following. Not all the items in the left-hand column can be matched; none is used twice.
w

		q
(a) Dreiser	5. *Our Finest Hour* _____	f
(b) Wright	6. *The Man with the Golden Arm* _____	
(c) Farrell	7. *1984* _____	
(d) Algren		
(e) Steinbeck	8. *An American Tragedy* _____	
(f) Churchill	9. *Witness* _____	
(g) Chambers	10. *Studs Lonigan* _____	
(h) Huxley		
(i) Orwell		
(j) Jefferson		
(k) Locke		

comprehension check: chapter 18

Write the letters of the best answers in the blanks. Key appears with Comprehension Check 16.

1. Every reader is a critic who evaluates literature in the light of:
   - (*a*) his own taste
   - (*b*) customary standards
   - (*c*) both of these
   - (*d*) neither of these

   a ✓

2. As a critical reader you will begin to see that:
   - (*a*) most critics are usually right
   - (*b*) authors are humans, too
   - (*c*) neither of these mentioned
   - (*d*) both *a* and *b*

   b

3. According to this chapter, an actor must read a Shakespearean play until:
   - (*a*) the groupings of the words come naturally
   - (*b*) the pronunciation of the words comes naturally
   - (*c*) the enunciation of the words comes naturally
   - (*d*) none of these

   a ✓

4. A good reader is not only a critic, he is also a:
   - (*a*) creator
   - (*b*) author
   - (*c*) playwright
   - (*d*) none of these

   a ✓

5. Creative and critical reading are the supreme test of a skillful reader because they:
   - (*a*) include every other reading skill
   - (*b*) make use of past experiences in life and books
   - (*c*) require an active and inquiring mind
   - (*d*) all of these

   d

6. The reader can share in Shakespeare's superb imagination when he:
   - (*a*) lets his own imagination grasp the play
   - (*b*) reads the play in the magnificent first folio edition
   - (*c*) reads the great critics on Shakespeare
   - (*d*) all of these

   a ✓

7. Being a critic means:
   - (*a*) condemning slowly (praising with faint damns)
   - (*b*) approving thoughtfully (damning with faint praise)
   - (*c*) examining carefully
   - (*d*) none of these

   c

8-10. (Choose the three best answers.) The duties of a critic, according to this chapter, are:
   - (*a*) reviewing the best books available to him
   - (*b*) finding exceptions to author's point of view
   - (*c*) establishing a reasonably broad cultural background
   - (*d*) reading *Canterbury Tales, Tom Jones,* and *The Odyssey*
   - (*e*) upholding democratic standards of taste established by custom
   - (*f*) checking generalizations against facts
   - (*g*) following the methods of John Ruskin and Matthew Arnold

   b
   c
   f

Margin letters: a, c, b, d, b, c, c, a, a, c

comprehension check: chapter 19

Write the letters of the best answers in the blanks. Key appears with Comprehension Check 21.

1. Many students object to analyzing a poem or story because:
   (a) the instrument of dissection is the mind
   (b) the authorship of a great work of literature is destroyed
   (c) a cold-blooded dissection destroys the beauty
   (d) it minimizes the liveliness of the work _b_ c ©

2. To understand and appreciate a book, a reader must:
   (a) know what the parts are
   (b) know the relationship of the parts
   (c) know what unites the parts
   (d) all of these _d_ c

3. When you strip the plot to its barest essentials, you should see:
   (a) its skeleton   (c) the essence of its parts
   (b) its good and bad parts (d) none of these _a_ b ©

4. When you go to a play you will notice that:
   (a) each act is a play in itself
   (b) the whole is divided into three parts
   (c) the actors' parts are integrated into the whole
   (d) all of these _a_ c ⓓ

Match the following. Not all the items in the left-hand column can be matched; none is used twice.

		f
(a) moves toward a goal	5. Willy Loman	____ d k
(b) Emily Dickinson	6. X-ray	____ i g d
(c) destroys beauty of organism	7. remark on dissecting insects	____ a f
(d) Alexander Pope	8. a very poor book	____ g a
(e) *Gone with the Wind*	9. a very good book	____ c e
(f) amoeba	10. girl meets boy theme	____
(g) determines arrangement of parts		
(h) top of head blown off		
(i) *Macbeth*		
(j) paramecium		
(k) fall from high estate		

comprehension check: chapter 20

Write the letters of the best answers in the blanks. Key appears with Comprehension Check 18.

c
1. The remarks of a "man who knows" carry authority because:
   (a) he has had wide and long experience
   (b) he has many influential friends
   (c) he observes sympathetically
   (d) all of these   *a*

d
2. You may infer that standards of judgment should represent:
   (a) the standards of custom
   (b) authoritative standards
b
   (c) the ideal toward which the performer strives
   (d) all of these   *c*

a
3. A standard of judgment mentioned in this chapter is:
   (a) legitimacy   (c) legality
   (b) legibility   (d) lexicography   *a* b

4. Characteristics of a book which must *not* hinder reading are:
   (a) type size   (c) color of page and print
   (b) size of margins   (d) all of these   *d*

b
5. When we read for knowledge it is sufficient if the author imparts information:
   (a) quickly   (c) smoothly
   (b) clearly   (d) all of these   *d* b

6. In a novel, the manner of expression must be:
   (a) mature, clear, and symbolic
d
   (b) appropriate, mature, and sensitive
   (c) clear, mature, and appropriate
   (d) all of these   *c*

b
7. The quotation about all words tending toward a pre-established design was by:
   (a) Edgar Lee Masters   (c) Edgar Allan Poe
   (b) Edgar Rice Burroughs   (d) Edward Guest   *c*

8. Most of the important standards of fiction are concerned with the effect of:
   (a) enrichment of life   (c) illuminating symbols
   (b) historical truth   (d) uplifting standards *a*

d
9. A reader must constantly ask if the author has provided:
   (a) a plausible plot and true-to-life characters
   (b) a real feeling of liveliness
d
   (c) suitable standards of design
   (d) subject not mentioned   *d* a

10. A work of fiction is as good or bad as:
    (a) the critics judge it   (c) you judge it
    (b) the author judges it   (d) subject not mentioned *d* c
b

comprehension check: chapter 21

Write the letters of the best answers in the blanks. Key appears with Comprehension Check 23.

1. Emerson said that to read well one must be braced by:
   (*a*) spirit and body   (*c*) labor and invention
   (*b*) joy and wisdom   (*d*) none of these   *d* – *c*

2. A great work of literature should be read the first time for:
   (*a*) a careful analysis   (*c*) fine points of characterization
   (*b*) subtle details of plot   (*d*) sheer enjoyment   *d*   c

3. Great literature is often:
   (*a*) an original communication   (*c*) philosophical in nature
   (*b*) a long and lively book   (*d*) all of these   *d* – *a*   d

4. Great literature requires the reader to:
   (*a*) meditate   (*c*) reread
   (*b*) brood   (*d*) all of these   *d*   c

Match the following. Not all the items in the left-hand column can be matched; none is used twice.

(*a*) inspired writing   5. written by Ruskin   *h*
(*b*) *Huckleberry Finn*   6. written by Emerson   *g* d
(*c*) Mark Twain   7. "A great book is something
(*d*) *Treasure Island*   everyone recommends and
(*e*) *Perpetual Books*   no one reads."   *c*   k l
(*f*) great literature should inspire 8. Emerson emphasized   *a*   g l
(*g*) *American Scholar*   9. Ruskin emphasized   *f*   d h
(*h*) *Sesame and Lilies*   10. classic American novel   *d*   f
(*i*) bring an active mind to reading   a
(*j*) Will Rogers   e
(*k*) *American Writer*
(*l*) a book perpetuates a truth an
     author has found

comprehension check: chapter 22

Write the letters of the best answers in the blanks. Key appears with Comprehension Check 20.

1. This chapter emphasizes reading poetry:
   (*a*) melodiously and clearly   (*c*) aloud
   (*b*) clearly and sensitively   (*d*) softly and warmly   _d_ c

a 2. Much verse is written in:
   (*a*) iambic pentameter   (*c*) blank verse
   (*b*) heroic couplets   (*d*) none of these mentioned   _d_

3. Poetry, like wine:
   (*a*) needs time to age   (*c*) is read with the blood of life
d (*b*) should be sipped and tasted   (*d*) provides warmth and strength   _b_

4. Something that brings an idea to life or drives home a startling insight is:
   (*a*) imagery   (*c*) innuendo and implication
   (*b*) rhythm and rhyme   (*d*) verse form, such as a sonnet or canto   _a_

d 5. In "Dirge" Kenneth Fearing says:
   (*a*) "Shafts of sunlight broke upon him"
   (*b*) "Zowie did he live and zowie did he die"
d (*c*) "The world is too much with us"
   (*d*) "Things are in the saddle and ride mankind"   _c_ b

6. When you read poetry, you should:
   (*a*) pounce on the rhyme word
   (*b*) bang out the rhyme word
d (*c*) raise your voice for the rhyme word
   (*d*) none of these   _d_

7. Two poets that expressed the same complaint were:
d (*a*) Fearing and Lindsay   (*c*) Pope and Poe
   (*b*) Emerson and Wordsworth   (*d*) none of these   _b_

8. This chapter implies or states that important things to consider when reading poetry are:
   (*a*) analysis and feeling
c (*b*) rhyme and rhythm
   (*c*) imagery and economy of expression
   (*d*) all of these   _c_ d

9. A poem should be read at:
   (*a*) 150 wpm   (*c*) 250 wpm
d (*b*) 200 wpm   (*d*) none of these mentioned   _d_

10. The meaning of a poem often comes:
    (*a*) through swift and sensitive analysis
c   (*b*) in waves of feeling
    (*c*) through sound and careful criticism
    (*d*) through attention to subtle details   _b_

c

comprehension check: chapter 23

Write the letters of the best answers in the blanks. Key appears with Comprehension Check 1.

1. Practice in oral reading will make you a better silent reader if you:
   (a) transfer your oral rate   (c) do not transfer your oral rate
   (b) read fast orally   (d) rate not mentioned   _d_   c

2. One great difference between the two types of reading is the:
   (a) audience   (c) effectiveness of the impact
   (b) analysis and criticism   (d) none of these   _a_   d

3. When you read orally, you:
   (a) read words in groups
   (b) look for the author's emphasis   a
   (c) never use a conversational tone
   (d) both a and b   _b d_

4. You do not stress *sung* in the sentence "The loveliest song I ever heard was sung   d
   by Lily Pons," because:
   (a) it precedes a prepositional phrase
   (b) it follows "was"
   (c) a characteristic of songs is to be sung   h
   (d) both a and b   _d_   g

5. In oral reading you stress:
   (a) the flourish that adds effectiveness
   (b) end words
   (c) idea-carrying words   c
   (d) concrete and relative words   _C_   i

6. This chapter says that in oral reading your eyes must: l
   (a) keep ahead of your voice   b
   (b) stay with your voice
   (c) keep on the audience as much as possible
   (d) function automatically on the reading matter and audience   _a_

7. It is good to read before an audience because you:
   (a) read aloud and hear your own voice
   (b) read slowly and carefully
   (c) make the meaning clear   _c_
   (d) practice good delivery   ____

8. Whether you express yourself orally or in writing, the unit of thought is:
   (a) each separate word   (c) concentrated in sentences   b
   (b) a phrase or word group   (d) concentrated in paragraphs   ____

9. Word groups are usually marked by:
   (a) punctuation   (c) paragraph division   d
   (b) grammatical structure   (d) both a and b   ____

10. When you stress implied words, you:
    (a) convey the meaning clearly   (c) subordinate unimportant details   a
    (b) attract favorable attention   (d) none of these   ____

what should be stressed in oral reading - T.

comprehension check: chapter 24

Write the letters of the best answers in the blanks. Key appears with Comprehension Check 22.

d
1. The two chief sources for reviews of contemporary books are:
   (a) major magazines and the Sunday edition of *The New York Times*
   (b) *The Book Review Digest* and *The Chicago Tribune*
   (c) Great Books Foundation and Classics Club
   (d) none of these   *b*

c
2. Most book critics:
   (a) get paid to praise
   (b) praise the majority of books they review
   (c) cannot be independent of the publisher who pays them
   (d) none of these   *d*

d
3. In addition to the *Bible*, the works of the following men have had the greatest influence on our time:
   (a) Darwin, Marx, Newton   (c) Darwin, Newton, Freud
c (b) Marx, Newton, Einstein   (d) Freud, Darwin, Marx   *c*

4. The mark of a well-educated man is his familiarity with:
   (a) his cultured friends   (c) the ideas in popular books
   (b) world problems and conditions (d) none of these   *d*

b
5. *The Book Review Digest*
   (a) is published every ten years
   (b) provides all critical opinion on a book
   (c) both of these
   (d) neither of these   *b*

c
6. *Good Reading* provides:
   (a) a test of "whodunits"   (c) reading for English teachers
   (b) the Great Books Foundation test (d) none of these   *d*

7. This chapter implies that the Great Books Foundation wants to:
   (a) present exciting reading material
b (b) make profits by educating the masses
   (c) stimulate, more than anything else, people's thinking
   (d) none of these   *c*

8. A book becomes great by its:
   (a) popularity with critics
d (b) conversational value among the best people
   (c) best-seller status
   (d) none of these   ____

9. The number of books published forces the reader to:
   (a) read efficiently   (c) select only the best books
b (b) read more frequently   (d) read as many reviews as possible   ____

10. This chapter implies that the ultimate purpose of this book is to:
    (a) teach efficient reading
a   (b) create a strong desire to read
    (c) encourage reading more good books
    (d) present all the important aspects of reading   ____

GRAPH OF PROGRESS IN RATE AND COMPREHENSION

DIRECTIONS: Record your rate (on the chart) and your comprehension (in the square above the chart) after you have read each chapter

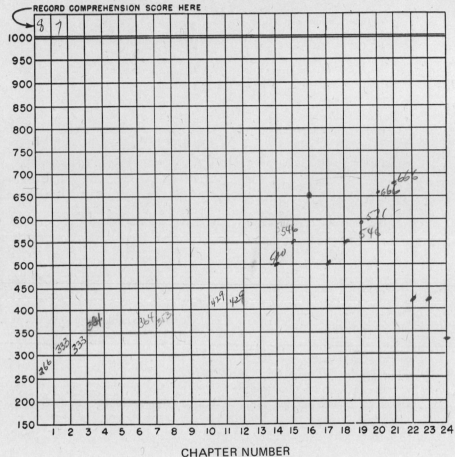

RECORD COMPREHENSION SCORE HERE

RATE IN WORDS PER MINUTE

CHAPTER NUMBER

TIME-RATE TABLE

Time in minutes and seconds converted to rate in words per minute.

Time	Rate	Time	Rate	Time	Rate	Time	Rate	Time	Rate
1:00	1000	2:00	500	3:00	333	4:00	250	5:00	200
1:05	933	2:05	481	3:05	324	4:05	245	5:05	197
1:10	857	2:10	461	3:10	316	4:10	240	5:10	194
1:15	800	2:15	445	3:15	308	4:15	235	5:15	192
1:20	752	2:20	429	3:20	299	4:20	230	5:20	188
1:25	704	2:25	415	3:25	290	4:25	225	5:25	184
1:30	666	2:30	400	3:30	281	4:30	221	5:30	180
1:35	633	2:35	384	3:35	276	4:35	218	5:35	178
1:40	602	2:40	376	3:40	271	4:40	215	5:40	176
1:45	571	2:45	364	3:45	266	4:45	211	5:45	172
1:50	546	2:50	353	3:50	260	4:50	208	5:50	170
1:55	524	2:55	343	3:55	255	4:55	204	5:55	168